120 BIBLE FACTS
Anyone Can Know

BY DON WAYNE KLINGER

120 Bible Facts Anyone Can Know

©2014 Don Wayne Klinger. All rights reserved.

PUBLISHED BY
Don Wayne Klinger
P.O. Box 342
Millersburg, PA 17061

PRINTED BY
CreateSpace, An Amazon.com Company

All Bible verses are from the
King James Version of the Bible.

120 BIBLE FACTS

Table of Contents

Acknowledgments		3
Preface		5
Chapter 1	7 Facts About the Bible	7
Chapter 2	7 Facts About God	23
Chapter 3	7 Facts About Jesus Christ	37
Chapter 4	7 Facts About the Holy Spirit	49
Chapter 5	7 Facts About Creation	61
Chapter 6	7 Facts About Sin	73
Chapter 7	7 Facts About Salvation	83
Chapter 8	7 Vocabulary Words of Salvation	95
Chapter 9	7 Blessings of Salvation	103
Chapter 10	7 Walks of the Believer	113
Chapter 11	7 Facts About Prayer	123
Chapter 12	7 Defenses of the Christian	133
Chapter 13	7 Facts About the Rapture of the Church	141
Chapter 14	7 Signs of the End Times	151
Chapter 15	7 Facts About the Tribulation	165
Chapter 16	7 Facts About the Millennium	177
Chapter 17	7 Facts About Heaven	185
Chapter 18	The Most Important Fact of All	189

120 BIBLE FACTS ANYONE CAN KNOW

Acknowledgments

I could not have done this book without the help of some very special people.

I have been teaching Bible for 50 years, and I thank the Lord Jesus Christ for giving me discernment and understanding of His Word.

The following individuals have been of great help and influence in completing this book:

Dr. Henry Morris of the Institute for Creation Research, who has greatly influenced my biblical worldview and understanding of creation.

Dr. Harold Willmington of Liberty University, who has increased my biblical knowledge by his teaching and lectures.

My daughter, Megan Etzweiler, who typed the manuscript in various forms.

Amy Smith, who gave valuable suggestions in the editing and publishing of this book.

120 BIBLE FACTS ANYONE CAN KNOW

120 BIBLE FACTS

Preface

In the Old Testament God called the Jews to be a witness and testimony for Him to all the countries round about them. What a blessing it was to serve the true and living God. But we know their hearts were far from Him. You can read their history in the Old Testament. The Bible tells us in Acts 2:36 that they killed the prophets, and they ended up rejecting and killing their promised Messiah of Genesis 3:15.

After the Cross, God established the church, which is still in existence today. God is now using the church to be a witness and testimony for Him during this Age of Grace. The Jews failed and have been sidetracked. They are not the primary means by which God is showing himself to the world today. God is working through His church.

In Acts 8 and 11, a great persecution of the church took place, and the church was scattered. The church went everywhere being a witness and testimony for Jesus. God still wants us to be a witness and testimony for Him. Not only pastors or assistant pastors or Sunday school teachers, He wants all members of the true church to witness and testify for His Son, the Lord Jesus.

Today we live in a fact-based society. People want to know the facts about everything. That's the way I am. Being an architect I have to know everything about everything.

In your everyday routine as you go through life rubbing elbows with people who don't know much about the Bible, many times God will open up conversations in which you can begin to discuss the Bible. Or maybe you are a person who just wants to know what the Bible says about various subjects. This book is for you as well. This book is written so it can be used to teach in a Sunday school class or a small group.

Here are Bible facts that everyone can know. Whether you go to church or not, you should know these Bible facts.

Altogether there are 18 subjects and 120 facts about these subjects that I will be covering.

All Bible verses are from the King James Version of the Bible.

CHAPTER 1 | **FACTS 1-7**

7 Facts About
The Bible

2 Timothy 3:16 says, "All Scripture is given by inspiration of God, and is profitable for doctrine, for reproof, for correction, for instruction in righteousness." All Scripture, that is inspired, that is God-breathed, has the Holy Spirit as its author. He told men what to write. The Bible nowhere claims to be written by inspired men; only holy men were the instruments used by the Holy Spirit to write it. The Bible is profitable. It will benefit you. It will profit your spiritual life.

The Bible is profitable for doctrine. It is what we believe and what we teach as church doctrine. It is profitable for reproof or to rebuke, to reprimand or convict not the mind but the heart. The Word will make a definite change or change you definitely. It is profitable for correction. It will make that which is wrong in your life right. It will restructure you and stabilize you.

You show me a weak, confused Christian, and I will show you a Christian who doesn't read the Word of God. The Bible is profitable for instruction in righteousness. It is a continuing teacher and will keep you tuned up and running in the right way, which is God's way. The Bible is a difficult book to understand; many people say that today.

1 Corinthians 2:13-14 says the natural man (the unsaved man — the person who has no concern about God) cannot discern the Word of God. He cannot understand it. When I study for a lesson, when I read the Bible, I always pray for the Holy Spirit to give me discernment so that I can understand the Word of God. If the Bible could be understood by natural men, it would only be a natural book and would not be the Word of God.

John 3:6 states, "That which is born of the flesh is flesh, and that which is born of the Spirit is spirit." Hebrews 4:12 says the Bible is a living word. It is real, it is true, and it is relevant for today. It is the Word of power over sin. It will strengthen, build you up, and give you confidence. It will divide and sever you from family, friends, and the world. It judges your innermost thoughts. It is the vehicle by which God deals directly with you through the Holy Spirit.

The Word of God examines, judges, and admonishes a person to holy living and to living faith. In the 18th century, the French infidel Voltaire predicted Christianity and the Bible would be completely forgotten in 100 years. He died in 1778, and since that time the world has been flooded with millions and millions of Bibles in scores of languages. Millions have come to know Christ as their own personal Savior. The Bible is the greatest book that has ever been written. I believe in all of the Bible from Genesis 1:1 to Revelation 22:21; it is inerrant (no mistakes). I believe it is infallible. In other words it will never be destroyed because God says "Heaven and earth shall pass away, but My words shall not pass away (Matthew 24:35). The Bible is God's way of revealing His Son, Jesus Christ, as Savior to a lost and dying world, so many men, women, boys, and girls can come to a saving knowledge of Jesus Christ.

The Bible is the foundation for Christianity. Romans 10:17 says, "Faith cometh by hearing, and hearing by the Word of God." The guideline for building a Christian life is the Bible. I believe in the inspiration of Scripture. It was inspired by Almighty God. Psalm 138:2 states that God has placed His Word above His name. Someone has said, "Read it to be wise, believe it to be saved, practice it to be right."

Here are seven facts about the Bible:

FACT 1 – The Bible has amazing unity.

Did you know 40 people wrote the Bible during a period of 1,500 years? They were people from different backgrounds and walks of life and 19 occupations. They were kings, a queen, prophets, soldiers, farmers, scribes, a tax collector, a physician, a fisherman, a carpenter, and a tent maker. It was written in 11 different places and in 10 different styles. The writers spoke in different languages and lived in different times and countries.

After knowing all these facts, what would be the chance of this book becoming a moral, scientific, prophetic, historical, and life-changing book? The answer is obvious: not one in a million. And yet the Bible perfectly dovetails together in perfect unity and harmony to give us the greatest book that has ever been written and that only God could supernaturally inspire.

FACT 2 – The Bible came into being by revelation, inspiration, and illumination.

Everybody knows the Bible has been and continues to be the world's best seller, but not everybody knows how this amazing book came down to us today. God used three wonderful methods as he carefully carved and gave mankind this book.

The first method He used is known as **revelation**. This is when God reveals to man what He wants written. Around 1400 B.C., God began to quietly call some 40 men and women into His presence. He did not call them all at once. In fact, it took Him more than 1,500 years to complete this job. He spoke to them the Scriptures that He wanted all of mankind to know.

Hebrews 1:1 tells us He spoke to the fathers and prophets in many ways. He often spoke to them by angels, which are God's messengers. Sometimes He spoke in a loud voice. He spoke directly to Adam, Noah, Abraham, Moses, Joshua, and others. Sometimes He spoke in a still, small voice. He used nature to speak to them. He used animals. He spoke through dreams. He used visions. He spoke through Christophany, which is a pre-Bethlehem appearance of Christ. This is spoken of in Scripture as the Angel of the Lord. When He had finished this speaking, the first method of carving out the Bible was complete. Revelation had occurred.

The second method God used is known as **inspiration**, which is from man to paper. In this method God inspired men to write what God wanted written. Down through the years, men have had various theories of inspiration. They have the *natural theory*, which says the Bible writers were inspired in the same sense that Shakespeare was inspired. In 2 Peter 1:20 we learn that Scripture did not come to us by private interpretation. Then there is the *mechanical theory*, which says God coldly dictated the Bible to His writers as you would dictate a letter to a secretary. Then came the *content theory*, which says only the main thoughts of a paragraph or chapter are inspired. Matthew 5:18 says, "One jot or one tittle shall in no wise pass from the law, till all be fulfilled."

Then men developed the *partial theory*, which says only certain parts are inspired. Liberal theology attests to this idea. Liberal theology is all about love and all about brotherhood. It opposes sin, righteousness, and judgment. Yet 2 Timothy 3:16 says, the Bible is "profitable for doctrine, for reproof, for correction, for instruction in righteousness."

Another theory was the *spiritual rule only*. Only religious matters such as ethics and spiritual values are inspired; historical and scientific matters are not inspired.

The final theory is *plenary verbal inspiration*. This theory is what born again Christians believe. The Bible has been inspired by God. In the Greek the word for inspiration is *theopneustos*, which means it is *God-breathed*. The first word of 2 Timothy 3:16 is "all." That means that all the 66 books of the Bible are inspired. All of the 1,189 chapters are inspired. All of the 31,173 verses of those 1,189 chapters of those 66 books are God-breathed.

When God created Adam, He took the dust of the ground, and He shaped and formed it into Adam. Then He breathed into Adam's nostrils the breath of life, and Adam became a living person. In the same way God breathed upon the words of the Scriptures, and the Scriptures now are the Living Word of God. The Bible strongly claims this fact.

2 Peter 1:21 states, "For the prophecy came not in old times by the will of man: but holy men of God spake as they were moved by the Holy Ghost."

Hebrews 4:12 says, "For the Word of God is quick, and powerful, and sharper than any two edged sword ...." I can objectively and unequivocally state without a shadow of a doubt that from Genesis 1:1 to Revelation 22:21, all of the 774,747 words have been inspired, or breathed by Almighty God. Plenary verbal inspiration assures us that God included all of the necessary things He wanted us to know and excluded everything else.

2 Timothy 3:15-17 tells us, "And that from a child thou (Timothy) hast known the holy Scriptures, which are able to make thee wise unto salvation through faith which is in Christ

Jesus. All Scripture is given by inspiration of God, and is profitable for doctrine, for reproof, for correction, for instruction in righteousness: That the man of God may be perfect, thoroughly furnished unto all good works."

God did not hyperbolize the Bible. He did not exaggerate Scripture to make it more interesting to the reader so that it cannot be taken literally. God meant what He said, and it happened exactly the way He said it. When the plain sense of Scripture makes common sense, then we are to seek no other sense.

Is inspiration still going on today? Has God inspired the writings of a 67th book of the Bible? For more than 2,000 years, evangelical Christians everywhere have held the belief that when the Apostle John wrote Revelation 22:21 and wiped his pen, inspiration stopped, and we were warned not to add or subtract from these writings (the Bible).

It is of utmost importance that we clearly understand this fact or else three tragic conclusions might be reached. The first one is God could have inspired the writings of others, such as Joseph Smith, founder of the Mormons; or Mary Baker Eddy, founder of Christian Science; or Charles Russell, founder of Jehovah's Witnesses. The second erroneous conclusion is that perhaps we still do not possess all of the details of salvation. And lastly, we might conclude that God allowed millions of devoted and faithful Christians to believe a lie for some 2,000 years. Of course, we know these three conclusions are not true because we know it is impossible for God to lie.

The third method God used and is still using is *illumination.* This is the transfer from paper to heart. Illumination is the method used by the Holy Spirit to shed divine light upon all seeking people as they look into the Word of God. Many times when I am reading Scripture and when I am trusting in the Spirit of God to reveal truth to me, I am illuminated. I find things that I've never known before in the Word of God. Illumination is necessary because of man's natural blindness. Remember 1 Corinthians 2:14 says, "But the natural man receiveth not the things of the Spirit of God: for they are foolishness unto him: neither can he know them, because they are spiritually discerned." Illumination also is necessary because of the blindness caused by Satan. 2 Corinthians 4:4 says, "The god of this world hath blinded the minds of them which believe not."

The results of illumination are twofold. First of all, sinners are saved. Psalm 146:8 says, "The Lord openeth the eyes of the blind." Psalm 119:130 says, "The entrance of thy words giveth light."

Secondly, Christians are strengthened. 1 Peter 2:2 tells us, "As newborn babes, desire the sincere milk of the Word, that ye may grow thereby." And Psalm 119:105 says, "Thy word is a lamp unto my feet, and a light unto my path." When you read and study the Bible, you have a better perspective on life, and it gives you a better direction.

Matthew 4:4 states, "Man shall not live by bread alone, but by every word that proceedeth out of the mouth of God." And John 20:31 states, "But these things are written, that ye might believe that Jesus is the Christ, the Son of God." 2 Timothy 2:15 tells us to, "Study to shew thyself approved unto God, a workman that needeth not to be ashamed, rightly dividing the Word of truth." The Holy Spirit uses the aid of believers in illuminating the hearts of others.

FACT 3 – The Bible is supernaturally indestructible.

A story is told that a visitor toured a blacksmith shop and seeing heaps of discarded hammers but only one used anvil, he asked the blacksmith, "How often do you replace the anvil?" The blacksmith replied, "Never. It's the anvil that wears out the hammers." And so it is with the Bible. The hammers of persecution, ridicule, criticism, disbelief, evolution, humanism, liberalism, and intellectualism, have for centuries pounded their vicious blows on this divine anvil but to no avail. It still stands unbroken, unshaken, unchipped.

In A.D. 303 Diocletian, a Roman ruler, said, "Extinct is the name of Christians." He had burned all the Bibles he could get his hands on. Twenty years later, Constantine, another Roman emperor, took office, and he offered a reward for any remaining Bibles that could be found. Within 24 hours 50 Bibles were brought to his throne room.

In 1199, Pope Innocent III ordered the burning of all Bibles. William Tyndale, in 1536 as he was being burned at the stake by the Bishop of London for printing and circulating the New Testament, cried, "Lord open the King of England's eyes!" Some 75 years later, King James of England had the Bible translated into the English language by the most noted scholars of the day, and thus we now have the King James Version of 1611. This Bible has made the greatest impact on humanity and has advanced the Gospel and God's program more than any other Bible ever written.

Voltaire, the French atheist, stated, "Another century and there will be no more Bibles left on the earth." After he died his printing press and house were purchased by the Geneva Bible Society and made into a Bible depot.

Many others have tried to destroy the Bible but to no avail. The Bible still stands.

FACT 4 – The Bible is historically and scientifically accurate.

The science of archeology has proved again and again the historical accuracy of the Bible. In Genesis 2 we find that the Garden of Eden was in the Tigris River Valley. Archeologists claim this area to be the cradle of civilization, where civilization began.

Then we have the fact of the universal flood in Genesis 6 and 7. Every race on earth has a record of a great flood. Dr. Harold Willmington has a friend named Rod Wallace, a missionary serving with New Tribes Mission. He began working among the people in the highlands of Papua New Guinea and was the first white man to ever set foot in that area. He spent many years learning the language and discovered to his astonishment that they had a detailed record of the flood.

The Tower of Babel mentioned in Genesis 11 is another example. Did you know archeologists have uncovered more than 24 ziggurats? These were towers built to worship the stars, sun, and moon and were first built by Nimrod (Genesis 10 and 11).

The fall of Jericho is another one. Joshua 6:1-5 tells us, "Now Jericho was straitly shut up because of the children of Israel; none went out, and none came in. And the Lord said unto Joshua, 'See I have given into thine hand Jericho, and the king thereof, and the mighty men of valour. And ye shall compass the city, all ye men of war, and go round about the city once. Thus shalt thou do six days. And seven priests shall bear before the ark seven trumpets of rams' horns: and the seventh day ye shall compass the city seven times, and the priests shall blow with the trumpets. And it shall come to pass, that when they make a long blast with the rams' horn, and when ye hear the sound of the trumpet, all the people shall shout with a great shout; and the wall of the city shall fall down flat, and the people shall ascend up every man straight before him.'"

When archeologists excavated the city of Jericho, they found the walls had fallen out flat and down the hill. If it would have been taken another way, perhaps with a battering ram, the walls would have fallen on top of each other and maybe fallen inside. Both the Scriptural account and the archeological evidence show that the walls of Jericho fell out flat and down the hill.

Another fact is Ahab's ivory palace as found in 1 Kings 22:39. Archeologists have uncovered his palace. Then there is his wife Jezebel, who was a Baal worshiper. God hated her very much because she turned the house of Israel to worshipping idols. In 2 Kings 9:30, Jehu, who was a general coming back from a battle, entered the city where Jezebel was living. Jezebel painted herself, put makeup on her face, and she stood in the window to confront Jehu. Jehu saw her, and he had two eunuchs in that house throw her out of the window down onto the street. Jehu later told men to go get her body and bury her. When they went, they could not find her because the dogs had eaten her. They only found her skull, her feet, and the palms of her hands, again, attesting to the fact of what Elijah said in 1 Kings 21:23 about dogs eating Jezebel. The fact here is that these archeologists, when they were digging there, found the cosmetic box that Jezebel used to paint herself for Jehu in 2 Kings 9:30.

Then there was the repentance of Nineveh in Jonah's day. In Jonah 4 this whole city repented, which was a great blessing unto the Lord. Nineveh was the capital of the Assyrian Empire and was founded by Nimrod in Genesis 10. It is about 300 miles north of Babylon. History shows that during the reign of Shalmaneser, the second king of Nineveh, there was a sudden change in religious worship. The Ninevites had worshipped many gods, and this stopped. They began to worship only one God. This attests to the fact of Jonah's preaching of repentance unto God and the whole city accepting God as the true and only God.

Many factors unite in certain assurance that the Bible is true. These factors include: the scientific accuracy in the Old Testament Scriptures, the testimony of the Passover, the unanimous acceptance by the early Christians and their Jewish contemporaries, the careful linguistic studies of dedicated and highly skilled conservative Bible scholars, the penetrating discoveries of archeology, the impact of the Old Testament on all subsequent world history, and the full confirmation by the Lord Jesus Christ of its historic and divine trustworthiness.

The Bible also attests to the fact that the world is round. Isaiah 40:22 says, "It is he that sitteth upon the circle of the earth." If only Magellan would have read this, he would not have had to set sail. Back in medieval times, people believed the earth was on the back of a large turtle that was trodding slowly through a cosmic sea. Here again, if only they had read Job 26:7, which says, "He stretcheth out the north over the empty places, and hangeth the earth upon nothing."

Another fact is the stars are innumerable, which we find in Genesis 15:5 when God told Abraham to look toward Heaven and see if he could number the stars. Astronomers using the Hubble telescope found that out in space there are millions and millions of stars. Scientists said there are as many stars out there as the sands in the sea, which the Scriptures proclaim (Genesis 22:17). And of course, all living things are produced after their kind (Genesis 1:21-26). This was proved by Louis Pasteur.

Then we come to scientific laws. The First Law of Thermodynamics states that energy has been created, and there is no new energy being created. This is from the Scriptures when God created the earth in six days, and on the seventh day He rested. He looked at His creation, and He was well pleased with what He had created. So God rested, and thus there is no more creation going on.

The Second Law of Thermodynamics, the Law of Entropy or the Law of Decay, states this old earth is slowly decaying. It is wound up like a clock and slowly running down. We find that true in our own lives. If you have a home that has any wood that's been on it for years and years, you find out that wood eventually decays. If our engines in our cars would only run forever, but they wear out just like this old earth.

FACT 5 – The Bible is prophetically accurate.

Prophecy is the foretelling of future events. One-fourth of all the Bible is prophecy. One only needs to study the history of the nation of Israel to see all the biblical prophecy that was fulfilled concerning it. The book of Daniel records the prophecy of the Gentile nations that would come in the world: Babylonia, Medo-Persia, Greece, Rome, and the other nations represented by clay, stone, and iron. These nations (empires) have all been great Gentile nations on the earth. History records these facts.

Then there is Daniel's "70th week." We know that each "week" in Daniel equals seven years and that 69 "weeks" have passed. That means 483 years are already fulfilled. We are waiting and looking for the last "week," which is seven years, the seven-year Tribulation, which will come on this earth in the future.

Also you have the "last days" prophecy. The increase of wars and rumors of wars is mentioned in Matthew 24:6. The world has only had 268 years of peace in the last 4,000 years. People will be covetous and engage in extreme materialism. They will be lovers of themselves more than lovers of God. They will engage in lawlessness and turn against one another. They will be cold and indifferent, as stated in 2 Timothy 3:2-4.

There is the overpopulation problem. Between 1850 and 1930, the world had between 1 and 2 billion people. Now in the year 2014, the world has more than 7 billion people. Those figures show a great increase of population. An increase of speed and knowledge, as stated in Daniel 12:4, also is taking place.

In 1680, Isaac Newton, the great Christian scientist, said that at some time in the future man is going to perhaps travel at 40 or 50 miles per hour. Of course, Voltaire, the atheist, said, "You see what Christianity makes out of a fine mind as Isaac Newton's. Why if man would travel 40 or 50 miles an hour, his breath would be taken away from him. His eyeballs would pop out on his cheeks."

We are living in the age of great knowledge with our computers and the Internet, but with it has come a departure from the Christian faith. Since 1950, great decline has occurred in the Christian faith due to evolution, humanism, and intellectualism.

Another sign of the last days is intense demonic activity. In the last days people are going to depart from the faith giving heed to seducing spirits, and they will be like clouds blown about with every wind of doctrine (1 Timothy 4:1). Many people believe in astrology and look in the paper every day to see what is going to happen in their lives.

Another sign is the unification of the one-world government (Revelation 13). The United Nations is the spearhead of this. We also see the unification of the world religious systems. We have the National Council of Churches and the World Council of Churches spearheading this, and, of course, the ecumenical movement is going on right now.

FACT 6 – The Bible has universal influence and circulation.

Western civilization is founded directly upon the Bible and its teachings. The Apostle Paul, instead of heading east to Asia, went west to Europe where he proclaimed and spread the Gospel.

The world's calendar and most holidays stem from the Bible.

The Bible has influenced the advancement of fine art. Some 52 famous Old Testament-themed and 65 famous New Testament-themed paintings are preserved in every important museum on the earth. They were painted by great artists such as da Vinci, Rembrandt, Michelangelo, Raphael, and others.

The Bible has produced more inspiring music than any other one thing on the earth, by far surpassing the music of Bach, Beethoven, and The Beatles.

The Bible has influenced our laws and led to the founding of our country by the Puritans and the Pilgrims. They all came here because of the Bible. Our Founding Fathers used biblical language. The charter of every colony includes biblical language. The Liberty Bell bears Scripture: Leviticus 25:10, "Proclaim liberty throughout all the land..."

Our presidents are still sworn into office by placing their right hand upon the Bible. Our most important buildings and monuments display Scriptural truth. The American public school system has roots in the Bible. It all started through the Sunday school movement in England.

Some 95 percent of our great colleges and universities were founded on biblical principles. Of the first 10, nine were founded by churches.

The American Bible Society and the Gideon's have distributed millions upon millions of Bibles all over the world, and they continue to do so today. During the U.S. Civil War, the American Bible Society produced 7,000 Bibles a day for both sides.

Abraham Lincoln said, "The Bible has shaped the advancement of the republic. The Bible and morality are the foundations of freedom."

No other ancient book can even remotely be compared with the Bible and its circulation.

FACT 7 – The Bible has life-changing power.

Undoubtedly, the greatest proof of the Bible's authenticity is its amazing ability to change corrupt and sinful humanity. The story is told of a socialist in New York pointing to an old, ragged street person and proudly announcing, "Socialism will put a new suit on that old man over there." A Christian rapidly proclaimed, "The Bible will put a new man in that old suit of clothes on that old man over there."

Millions upon millions of people have been changed by the Bible. Think of your own life and how it has changed you. If you haven't been changed, read the Bible and believe it, and you will be changed for the good. The Bible is not the product of human expression and experience nor is it teaching religious speculations or man's supposed encounters with God. It is the breath of God, the very words of God to mankind. It would be no different if God had penned it Himself. In the coming judgment, it will be far easier to explain to God why we had too much faith in His Word, the Bible, than too little.

CHAPTER 2 | FACTS 8-14

7 Facts About
God

Has anyone ever asked you where God came from? They have asked me that many times. My answer is that He always was. God was always there. The Bible doesn't tell us where He came from. There are many Scriptures assuring us that God has always been. For instance Psalm 93:2 says, "Thy throne is established of old: thou art from everlasting." In Isaiah 40:28 it reads, "He is the everlasting God, the Lord." Psalm 90:2 states, "Before the mountains were brought forth, or ever thou hadst formed the earth and the world, even from everlasting to everlasting, thou art God."

One of the things we know about God is that He inhabits eternity (Isaiah 57:15). He is the Alpha and Omega, the beginning and the end (Revelation 1:8). The most glorious fact of all is that this living God also became man in the person of the Lord Jesus Christ. Jesus said, "Ye have neither heard His voice at any time, nor seen His shape" (John 5:37). In John 14:9 Jesus says, "He that hath seen me, hath seen the Father." The Bible reveals God as the only infinite and eternal being, having no beginning and no end. He is creator, and He is sustainer of all things. He is the supreme personal intelligence and righteous ruler of His universe. He is life, and therefore, the only source of life. Man is natural and cannot know God by wisdom. God has revealed Himself in the Old Testament by the prophets and in the New Testament by His Son Jesus Christ. In fact, the writers of both the Old and New Testaments believed the fact that God exists.

I want to give you seven facts about God.

FACT 1 – God was in the beginning.

God was the beginner. The first chapter of the first book of the Bible begins with these four words: "In the beginning God..." The Bible nowhere attempts to explain or tell us where God came from. It nowhere attempts to even prove or argue the existence of God. It just makes this profound statement that God was in the beginning and expects the reader — that's us — to accept it as fact. God was always there. He is the Alpha and Omega, the beginning and the end. Before anything was made, He was, and He that was, made all that is. The fact of God and the nature of God is clearly declared in the following Bible verses: Psalm 19:1 and John 1:18.

"The fool hath said in his heart, There is no God" (Psalm 14:1). So belief, that's faith, is the underlying principle and truth of the Bible. Hebrews 11:6 says, "But without faith it is impossible to please Him: for he that cometh to God must believe that He is."

And so we find beyond the shadow of a doubt that God was in the beginning. We will talk about this more when we get into the seven facts of creation.

FACT 2 – God is Spirit.

John 4:24 says, "God is a Spirit: and they that worship Him must worship Him in spirit and in truth." As soon as you talk about spirits, people visualize some disembodied person floating around in space in an eerie and scary setting. How do you picture God? Do you picture Him as an old, gray-haired, bearded man with a big finger? When the Bible talks about worshipping God in the Spirit, it is not talking about great spiritual experiences. It is the sense of knowing and loving God. It is a sense of knowing His awareness in your life. We are trichotomous, which means there are three parts to our makeup. Paul says in 1 Thessalonians 5:23 that we have a body, a soul, and a spirit. When we bury someone, we never bury a person; we bury a body. We bury their body because their soul and spirit go to be with the Lord immediately. When Adam, being our human representative, sinned against God, our spirit became dormant. In other words, it became inactive toward God. We became a natural person, and we became unconcerned about spiritual things, about the things of God (1 Corinthians 2:14). But when you got saved, that dead, dormant spirit was quickened. It was made alive. It was revitalized. It was regenerated.

Can you remember when you got saved? Can you remember who you were before salvation and after salvation? That is regeneration of the spirit in your body. You now have a new spirit. Through the spirit, you now know God. You become aware of His presence. I remember when I was unsaved I couldn't have cared less about God. I didn't even think about Him. But when you get saved your spirit bears witness with His Spirit that you are His child. You now have a spiritual connection with God. He becomes your heavenly Father. You and God can communicate one with another; we call this prayer.

Genesis 1:27 says, "So God created man in His own image, in the image of God created He him; male and female created He them." I doubt that we look like God because I think that our sin has marred that image that Adam had in the beginning. What are we going to look like in heaven? I believe we are going to be a spiritual, heavenly being. We will look like we do now. After Jesus was crucified, He appeared to Mary Magdalene in bodily form, and Mary knew Him. After that, He appeared to the disciples and to Thomas in a bodily form, and they knew Him (John 20:19-29).

In Luke 16 we have the account of the rich man and the poor man, Lazarus. Lazarus would lay at the gate of the rich man and beg for food as the rich man passed by. Eventually, they both died. It doesn't give this in the account of Scripture, but it leads you to believe that somewhere in his life, this poor man, Lazarus, accepted Christ as his Savior. Both men went to Sheol. Old Testament Sheol is a place in the center of the earth. It has two areas, one called Hades (Hell) and the other Paradise (Abraham's Bosom). Hades is where unbelievers go, and Paradise is where believers go.

There is a great gulf between Hades and Paradise, and no one from either side can cross over. In Old Testament times, this is where everybody's soul and spirit went. In fact, everybody who is an unbeliever, who has never received Christ as their Savior, still goes to Hades today. When Christ died on the Cross of Calvary, He went down to Paradise in the center of the earth and got all of the saved people (all those who believed in Him). He took them to Heaven. Ephesians 4:8-9 says He moved Old Testament Paradise up to Heaven. Now when we pass on, if we do, our soul and our spirit will go up to Paradise. If you have never received Christ as your Savior, your spirit and soul will go to Hades in the center of the earth, down with the rich man.

As that rich man was down there, he looked across this great gulf that was fixed between, and he saw Lazarus. He had his five senses about him; he could see Lazarus. The Bible tells us that the rich man was tormented in the flames. He wanted Jesus or God to have Lazarus dip his finger in water and bring one drop of water the whole way across the great gulf so this rich man could stick his tongue out and have Lazarus drop the one drop of water on his tongue. This is not a story; it is biblical. This is not a parable. This really happened. But God said to the rich man, "I cannot let Lazarus cross this great gulf. You made your decision, and Lazarus made his decision."

The rich man then said, "I have five brothers up there on earth. Would you send Lazarus back and tell my five brothers about this place? Tell them to accept your Son Jesus. Would you have him do this?" And God's answer was, "No, I will not do that because they have the Scriptures. That is why I gave them the Scriptures, so they have a witness and testimony of Me. They have prophets up there to tell them."

This puts a burden on us to be a witness and testimony to our families, our friends, all the people whom we know to tell them about our wonderful Savior, the Lord Jesus Christ. But the fact I want you to see is that the rich man saw Lazarus exactly the way he was on earth.

I am saying by this Scripture, you are going to look just like you look now. We are going to know each other, but we are going to be in a different, spiritual body. In 2 Corinthians 12:2, the Apostle Paul was called up into Heaven. When he got there, he looked at himself and said, "I can't tell whether I am in the body, or I am in the spirit." He looked like he did down on earth. He said this two times. Based on this, I conclude the fact that we are going to look just like we do now, but we are going to have these marvelous, wonderful, spiritual bodies to live in.

FACT 3 – God has three distinct personalities.

We call this the trinity (three persons in one). Although the word "trinity" is not specifically used in the Bible, a number of Scripture verses denote God's plurality (more than one). In Genesis 1:1, the Hebrew word for God is *Elohim*, which is in the plural tense and reveals the plurality of God. The word is used some 2,570 times in the Old Testament.

In Genesis 1:26 the plurality of God is used three times, "Then God said, 'Let *Us* make man in *Our* image, according to Our likeness; let them have dominion over the fish of the sea, over the birds of the air, and over the cattle, over all the earth and over every creeping thing that creeps on the earth.'" This is the dominion mandate, but the point here is the words "Let *Us* make man in *Our* image, according to *Our* likeness." The plurality of God is given here as the trinity.

Genesis 3:22 says, "And the Lord God said, 'Behold, the man is become as one of us, to know good and evil: and now, lest he put forth his hand, and take also of the tree of life, and eat and live forever.'" Again, plural in number. Further on in Genesis 9 right after the flood, Noah came off of the ark on Mount Ararat with his three sons, Shem, Ham, and Japheth. God's command to them was "I want you to go and spread over the earth. I want you to replenish the earth. Repopulate the earth."

You also find the account of a man named Nimrod in Genesis 10. Nimrod is called "the Apostate," which means *turning away from revealed truth*. Today we have a lot of churches that once preached the Gospel, but no longer do so, no longer believe in the Gospel, and have turned away from the revealed truth. I went to an apostate church. The preachers no longer preached the Gospel and didn't believe in Jesus, so I got away from there.

Nimrod the Apostate was turning people away from the revealed will of God. He was having them worship idols. He was having them do everything but worship the true and living God. His kingdom was Babel, and the city that he founded was Babylon. He was going to build a tower up to the heavens away from any floods that might come on the earth again. He was going to show that he was better than God. In fact, this tower was known as a ziggurat. You can go over to Iraq, and you can find foundations for these ziggurats that they were building way back some 4,500 years ago. Nimrod was going to build this tower. God says in Genesis 11:5-7, "And the Lord came down to see the city and the tower, which the children of men builded." Now this was against God. God didn't want them to do this. God's command was: "Get out of here and spread over the earth." "And the Lord said, Behold the people is one, and they have all one language; and this they begin to do: and now nothing will be restrained from them, which they have imagined to do. Go to, let *Us* go down, and there confound their language, that they may not understand one another's speech."

What we have here in the Scriptures is that God has three distinct personalities known as God the Father, God the Son, and God the Holy Spirit. Jesus is the only begotten Son of God. In other words the word *begotten* means *He came out of the Father* (John 1:13). The Holy Spirit proceeded out of the Father and the Son (John 15:26).

As an architect, I can give you this dimensional example of the trinity. Let's look at a Bible. A Bible has height, depth, and width. They cannot be separated, yet they are not the same. In the unity of the Godhead, there are three distinct, eternal, and holy persons, God the Father, the Son, and the Holy Spirit. They cannot be separated, yet they are not the same. We call this the trinity.

FACT 4 – God has three distinct attributes.

First, God is **omniscient,** which means He knows all things. You can't "get away with anything" with God. His eyes are upon the righteous, so don't think that you can do things, and no one will ever know. God knows because of His omniscience. He knows if a sparrow falls to the ground. He possesses complete and universal knowledge. The eyes of the Lord are in every place, and the ways of a man are before the Lord. He knows our thoughts, our words, and our needs. He knows our sorrows and our deeds. He knows our foolishness and our frailties. He knows our devotion to Him. He knows all of those who are His. He truly is all-knowing.

The second attribute of God is He is **omnipresent**. He is everywhere at the same time with His whole being. He is different from the devil. The devil is not omnipresent. The devil cannot be everywhere at one time. He can only be at one place at one time, but the devil has fallen angels. In fact, one-third of all the angels in Heaven sided with his rebellion against God and became demons. So the devil has millions of demons all around in the air that we cannot see. They are always after us. They try to get us to rebel against God. They try to get us to deny the God of creation. That is how they act, but they are not the devil. They are his helpers. But God is omnipresent. He is everywhere. He penetrates and fills the universe in all of its parts. His presence is in the world acting within and through His creation.

Proverbs 15:3 tells us, "The eyes of the Lord are in every place beholding the evil and the good." This God who created and made all things is not only omniscient, He is omnipresent. 2 Chronicles 16:9 says, "For the eyes of the Lord run to and fro throughout the whole earth, to shew himself strong in the behalf of them whose heart is perfect toward him."

David was right when he wrote Psalm 139:8-12. He said, "If I ascend up into Heaven, thou art there: if I make my bed in hell, behold thou art there. If I take the wings of the morning and dwell in the uttermost parts of the sea; Even there shall Thy hand lead me, and Thy right hand shall hold me. If I say, surely the darkness shall cover me; even the night shall be light about me. Yea, the darkness hideth not from Thee; but the night shineth as the day: the darkness and the light are both alike to Thee."

God's omnipresence should not be understood as pantheistic. Although he sees everyone and everything, He is not in everyone and everything. The creation did not create itself. In fact, God is above and beyond His creation.

The third attribute of God is He is ***omnipotent***, which means He is all-powerful. God is an omnipotent God. Jeremiah 32:17 says, "Ah Lord God! behold, Thou hast made the heaven and the earth by Thy great power and stretched out arm, and there is nothing too hard for Thee." When God told Sarah, who was 90 years old, that she was going to have a child, she began to laugh. God's response to Sarah was, "Is anything too hard for the Lord?" (Genesis 18:14). Many years later, the angel told the virgin Mary that she would have a son, and she said, "How shall this be, seeing I know not a man." And the angel replied, "For with God nothing shall be impossible" (Luke 1:34 & 37).

Some things God cannot do. He cannot be tempted with evil (James 1:13). He cannot lie (Titus 1:2). Whatever He does is right, and whatever He says is true. We may not always understand why He says or does something. But in eternity, we will learn that He was indeed able to do what He says. He is omnipotent. God created the cosmos or the universe in all of its microscopic complexities and all of the living kinds with their microscopic complexities. He says, "Behold, I am the Lord, the God of all flesh: is there any thing too hard for Me?" (Jeremiah 32:27).

We know that God is all-powerful. He can do all things and has created all that there is. He has numbered the stars and called them by name. Can you imagine that? Have you ever watched *Nova* and seen the Hubble telescope as it looked into space at all the stars? It is magnificent. You can look at the Milky Way on a really clear night. There are millions upon millions of stars all through the Milky Way, and God created every one of them. He has given every one a name. He is omnipotent.

He controls all things. He moves in the supernatural realm. This is the realm outside of our three-dimensional concept. This is beyond our natural knowledge. It is the realm of eternity with its endless space that has no bounds. This is God's habitation. It's where He lives.

FACT 5 – God is holy.

God is holy. He is hallowed. He is set apart from everyone and everything. There is no one like Him. That is why you hallow the name of God: "Hallowed be thy name" (Matthew 6:9). Did you ever think of what that word really means? It means He is set apart. He is perfect in all of His ways. There is no sin in Him. He is pure and free from all defilement. He is without blame. He is just in forgiveness and judgment. Holiness covers His moral and righteous nature. It covers His grace and His mercy. God would have us to seek after His holiness. We can then develop Christian character and be vindicated from every charge that might possibly be brought against us at the Judgment Seat of Christ (Romans 14:10 and 2 Corinthians 5:10). We will all stand at His judgment seat because of our failure to confess our sins to Him. Do you know if you confess your sins, He will forgive all your iniquities? He will remember your sins no more.

I keep telling people to be confessed up to date. Don't go through life thinking you are a sinless person. You are not sinless because we sin every day. If a person says they don't sin, they make Him a liar (1 John 1:10). Be careful because there are demons after us all the time. You do not know when you are going to be called home to be with God, and if you are confessed up to date as you stand before the Judgment Seat of Christ, you are going to be vindicated from your sins. I would hate to be standing up there with the whole church around the throne, and my sins be listed that I did on this earth. How embarrassing that would be. We need to be confessed up to date.

FACT 6 – God is sovereign.

This means that God is the absolute and sole ruler in and of the universe. He has all the power, all the knowledge, all the wisdom, and all the determination to carry out His will. Whatever he does is right by definition, and whatever He allows is for His holy purpose.

Romans 9:20 says, "Shall the thing formed say to him that formed it, Why hast thou made me thus?" He has a purpose for the world, and everything is going according to His will. Sometimes I might think, "Wait a minute God. What is going on here?" I have to get back into my Bible and remind myself everything is working according to His will. It may be moving slowly, but it is all according to His will.

All things happen according to His perfect plan. Nothing happens by chance. He allows and disallows. He controls the world's powers. He allows the powers that be. "The most High ruleth in the kingdom of men" (Daniel 4:17). Every time there is an election, if my man doesn't make it, I say it is still God's will. Maybe sometimes what we really want, we don't deserve, and God is not going to give it to us. His plan is to someday take all believers, that's the saved, to Heaven in what is known as the Rapture (1 Thessalonians 4). There will be seven years of tribulation on this earth when he will take vengeance on a Christ-denying world (Revelation 6-18). He will reclaim His chosen people, the Jews. He will bring all nations of the world to judgment (Matthew 25:32). He is going to set up His throne on this earth and rule for 1,000 years. "For the earth shall be filled with the knowledge of the glory of the Lord, as the waters cover the sea" (Habakkuk 2:14). He is going to judge all unsaved people at the Great White Throne Judgment (Revelation 20:15). He is going to give all believers a home in heaven to live with Him forever throughout all the ages of eternity (Revelation 21:10).

FACT 7 – God loves mankind.

According to 1 Timothy 2:4, God wants all men to be saved. Romans says His righteousness is for everyone. He continues to pursue us. He has no pleasure in the death of the wicked (Ezekiel 33:11). 1 John 4:16 says, "And we have known and believed the love that God hath to us. God is love; and he that dwelleth in love, dwelleth in God, and God in him." So it was not His omnipotence nor his omniscience that constrained Him to create man and woman in His image. It must have been His nature of love and His desire for fellowship.

Isaiah 43:7 says God has created us for His glory. Proverbs 16:4 tells us, "The Lord hath made all things for Himself." God is love, and He loves mankind. He not only planned a creation but also a plan of salvation. He saved us according to His own purpose and grace, which was given us in Christ Jesus before the world began. "Behold what manner of love the Father hath bestowed upon us" (1 John 3:1). God is indeed a God of love.

John 3:16 says, "For God so loved the world, that he gave His only begotten Son." Galatians 4:14 says, "But when the fullness of time was come, God sent forth His Son" because of His love for us. "The fullness of time" means a time when Israel had put away idolatry, the Old Testament revelation was complete, and synagogues had been built all throughout the region. All through Judea, the Jews were expecting the promised Messiah of Genesis 3:15. Religiously, Gentiles were hopelessly controlled by

Greek philosophies. They were deep into pagan mythology. They had immoral practices. They were in desperate need of a Savior. Politically, Rome had established a *Pax Romana*, in other words, a *Roman peace*. The Romans built a network of roads throughout the region to make travel to the cities safe. Roman law produced civil obedience, and Roman legions stationed throughout the area assured political stability. Socially the Greek culture and language had united the area making the proclamation of the Gospel easier. At this time God sent forth His Son, made of a woman, made under the law, to redeem us and adopt us as sons. God loved us before we loved Him. (1 John 4).

We were chosen by Him before the foundations of the world (Ephesians 1:4). We cannot elude the implications of these facts about God. Everywhere His identity is shown to us. We are surrounded by His glory. His majesty is written across the sky. He rides the wings of the wind. He sits in the most high and holy place. He inhabits eternity. His grace is greater than all of our sins. He is our heavenly Father. He is the Lord God Almighty.

CHAPTER 3 | FACTS 15-21

7 Facts About
Jesus Christ

Christianity differs from all other religions because it is more than a religion. It is the life of the living Son of God made living in your heart and mine. Christ is Christianity. Christianity is Christ. The word *Christian* comes from the phrase *Christ in*. A Bible-believing person, or a born-again person, has Christ in his or her heart. It is Christ in you, the hope of glory (Colossians 1:27).

If you have personally received Jesus Christ into your heart, you are a Christian. Christ dwells in you through the Holy Spirit. Receiving Christ is the only way you become a Christian. It is not by attending a church, living a good life, giving money to your church, being baptized when you were an infant, belonging to a church, coming from a Christian family, or living in a Christian nation.

Christianity is exclusive. Christians are exclusivists. We believe there is only one way to Heaven. Jesus is the only way. You must accept Him. It comes down to knowledge versus opinion.

I want to give you seven facts about the Lord Jesus Christ.

FACT 1 – Jesus was with the Father in the beginning.

Philippians 2:6 tells us, "Who, being in the form of God (we are talking about the Lord Jesus Christ), thought it not robbery to be equal with God: But made Himself of no reputation, and took upon Him the form of a servant and was made in the likeness of men: And being found in fashion as a man, He humbled himself, and became obedient unto death, even the death of the Cross." These verses are known as the *knosis* of Jesus. In verse seven, the word *made* is *keynew* in the Greek. It means to *empty oneself*. Christ did not empty Himself of the Godhead. He did not cease to be what He essentially and eternally was. The word "form" means He just took on a new outward appearance. He emptied and stripped Himself of the insignia of majesty and the outward and visible manifestation of the Godhead, but He never ceased to be God. This is known as *hyperstatic union*. He was as much God as if He had never been man and as much man as if He had never been God.

The Bible clearly gives the fact that Jesus was with God in the beginning and that He is the second person of the Godhead.

Colossians 1:16-17 says, "For by Him were all things created, that are in Heaven, and that are in earth, visible and invisible, whether they be thrones, or dominions, or principalities, or powers: all things were created by Him, and for Him. And He is before all things, and by Him all things consist." The first chapter of John's Gospel says, "In the beginning was the Word, and the Word was with God, and the Word was God. The same was in the beginning with God." Later in verse 14 we read, "And the Word was made flesh and dwelt among us." This is talking about Jesus. Again, in John 17:5, it says, "And now, O Father, glorify thou Me with Thine own self with the glory which I had with Thee before the world was." These Bible verses attest to the plurality of God when they use the word *us*. Jesus was the second person of *us*.

FACT 2 – Jesus was virgin born.

The Bible again tells us in Isaiah 7:14, "Therefore the Lord himself shall give you a sign; Behold, a virgin shall conceive, and bear a son, and shall call His name Immanuel." Jesus' birth was a miracle. It was the conception of Christ's earthly body. It was supernatural. It was unique. Matthew 1:24-25 tells us that Joseph "knew her not" until she brought forth her firstborn son and called his name Jesus. This is important that the Scripture brings this out. It attests to the fact that Mary was a virgin. She knew no man. The seed that was in her to bring forth her firstborn (not her second born or her third born) was placed in her by the Holy Spirit. God was very factual when He inspired the Scriptures.

This conception was miraculous, not immaculate. This idea of immaculate conception is a false, religious dogma that Mary was conceived and born without original sin. The Bible states very clearly that ***all*** have sinned, and by plenary verbal inspiration, that means Mary, too.

When Jesus joined himself to Mary's body, it was an everlasting arrangement, for He will continue to manifest Himself in this body throughout all the ages of eternity. When we see Jesus face to face, He will not be in an invisible, spiritual form.

Why the virgin birth? God never does anything without a good reason. I want to give you 11 reasons for the virgin birth.

1. **To reveal the invisible God.** God loved the world. How could He get His message across? He sent Jesus into the world to become man and tell God's story in man's language to reveal the invisible God.
2. **To fulfill the prophecy of Genesis 3:15** when God was in the garden after Adam and Eve sinned. He got Adam

and Eve and Satan together in the garden and told them that He promised that a Redeemer would come. This Redeemer was eventually going to be Jesus Christ, who would redeem man from his sinful nature.

3. **To make a sacrifice for sin.** Jesus left the ivory palaces of Heaven to come down to this world and enter Mary's womb to make a sacrifice for our sins. He, by the grace and will of God, tasted death for every man.

4. **To reconcile man to God.** God was in Christ reconciling the world to Himself. Not imputing or placing to our account our sin, but rather placing our sins to Christ's account. Thus we are justified before a holy and righteous God.

5. **To provide an example for believers.** Christ has come to be an example to all believers. After we are saved we study and follow the life of Christ because He is our example. We would have no example apart from the virgin birth of Christ.

6. **To be made our high priest,** who is now seated at the right hand of God the Father. By prayer he can be touched with all of our infirmities.

7. **To destroy the devil and his works.** He was obedient unto the death of the Cross that through death he might destroy him that had the power of death, that is the devil (Philippians 2:8).

8. **To heal the brokenhearted.** God sent Him "to heal the brokenhearted, to preach deliverance to the captives, and recovering of sight of the blind, to set at liberty them that are bruised" (Luke 4:18).

9. **To give life and abundant life.** He did not come as a thief to steal and kill and destroy, but He came that they might have life and have it more abundantly.

10. **To glorify the Father.** "And whatsoever ye shall ask in my name, that will I do, that the Father may be glorified in the Son" (John 14:13).
11. **To uphold the truth and validity of the Word of God.** In Jeremiah 22, God was going to give Israel (His people) into the hands of Nebuchadnezzar, king of Babylon. God said Coniah, or Jeconiah, the son of Jehoiakim, king of Judah, will never sit on the throne of David. Neither will any of his descendants sit on that throne. In Matthew 1 we read the lineage of Joseph. In verse 11 we read Jeconiah is part of this lineage, and in verse 16 we read that Joseph was of the lineage of Jeconiah. If Joseph would have had anything to do with the conception of Jesus, Jesus could not sit on the Throne of David and rule and reign on the earth during the Millennium. The Bible is very accurate with the facts it gives.

FACT 3 – Jesus was God in the flesh.

In the Old Testament we see man was made in the image of God (Genesis 1:27). In the New Testament we have God made in the image of man (Philippians 2:7). Jesus Christ was quintessentially God. He was the perfect manifestation and embodiment of God. Isaiah 7:14 says His name would be *Immanuel*, which means *God with us*. Isaiah prophesied this prophecy 700 years before Jesus came. Jesus' God-nature is well established in the Scriptures. John 1:1 says, "The Word was God." John 1:14 says, "The Word was made flesh" in the person of Jesus Christ. In John 20:28, Thomas calls Him, "My Lord and My God."

Again in John 8:58 Jesus said, "Before Abraham was, I am." God told Moses, "I am that I am" (Exodus 3:14). Colossians 1:14-15 says, "In whom we have redemption through His blood, even the forgiveness of sins: Who is the image of the invisible God, the first born of every creature."

FACT 4 – Jesus is the only Savior.

The angel of the Lord told Joseph to "call His name Jesus: for He shall save His people from their sins" (Matthew 1:21). The word *Jesus* means *Jehovah saves*. Isaiah 53:5-6 says, "But He was wounded for our transgressions, He was bruised for our iniquities: the chastisement of our peace was upon Him; and with His stripes we are healed. All we like sheep have gone astray; we have turned everyone to his own way; and the Lord hath laid on Him (that is Jesus) the iniquity of us all.

Peter said in Acts 4:12, "Neither is there salvation in any other: for there is none other name under Heaven given among men, whereby we must be saved." The Apostle Paul states in Romans 6:23, "For the wages of sin is death; but the gift of God is eternal life through Jesus Christ our Lord." He was the promised Redeemer of Genesis 3:15, and Colossians 1:14 tells us we are bought by His blood. Paul stated that Christ came into the world to save sinners. 1 John 2:2 says, "And he is the propitiation for our sins: and not for ours only, but also for the sins of the whole world." Here John uses an 85 cent word *propitiation*. *Propitiation* means that *He was the final atonement*. He was the final payment for sin. A holy and just God demanded a holy and just sacrifice. Jesus became that holy and just sacrifice, and Almighty God accepted it as the final payment for sin. Jesus is the way, the truth, and the life (John 14:6). Whosoever will call on the name of Jesus will be saved, and that is the Gospel truth.

FACT 5 – Jesus was sinless.

He knew no sin. 2 Corinthians 5:21 says, "For He hath made him to be sin for us, who knew no sin." 1 Peter 2:22 says, "Who did no sin, neither was guile found in his mouth." Hebrews 4:15 says, "For we have not an high priest which cannot be touched with the feeling of our infirmities; but was in all points tempted like as we are, yet without sin." He had no sin. 1 John 3:5 tells us, "He was manifested to take away our sins; and in Him is no sin."

His sinlessness was attested by Pilate when he said in John 9:6, "I find no fault in Him." So when we talk about sin, two words come to mind: *peccability* and *impeccability*. *Peccability* says Jesus could have sinned, and *impeccability* says Jesus could not sin. To suggest Jesus could have sinned is to disqualify Him as Savior. A peccable Christ would mean a peccable God. A God that could sin would not be a holy God, and therefore He would not be just in judging our sins. God's holiness is far more than the absence of sin. It is what we call positive virtue. To deny positive virtue is to deny the holy character of God. You see positive virtue has no room for sin. It is sinless.

The question comes to mind if Christ could not have sinned, then what was the purpose of His temptation in the wilderness? These temptations were not to see if Christ would sin; they were to prove He would not and could not sin.

FACT 6 – Jesus rose from the dead.

He is a resurrected, living Savior seated at the right hand of God and has become the believers' high priest. He is carrying out His three distinct functions of that office. The first function is as intercessor. He makes petitions and pleads for us in prayer before the Throne of God. His second function is as our mediator. He is our go between, the middle man between the believer and the Father. And His third function is as our chief advocate. He is our defense counsel as we are falsely accused before the throne by Satan himself.

No other doctrine in all of the Bible is so hated by Satan as the resurrection of Christ. Satan has attempted to ridicule it, down play it, deny it, or simply explain it away.

The devil has used many theories to deny the resurrection. He has used the **fraud theory**, which says that either Jesus or His disciples simply invented the resurrection account. Jesus studied the Old Testament regarding a Messiah and somehow arranged these accounts to be fulfilled by Himself. Thus the whole account of His resurrection was nothing but a big fraud. Another theory is the **swoon theory**. According to this theory, Christ only fainted on the Cross and was later revived by the cool air of the tomb. His disciples paid the Roman soldiers to open the tomb. The **vision theory** says the disciples used some kind of drug on the people at the Cross. Christ was never crucified; thus He was seen walking around bodily for 40 days after the resurrection. Another theory, the **spirit theory**, says only His spirit arose, and His body is still in the grave. The **heart theory** says we are to believe He was only resurrected in the hearts of His friends, but they recorded it in the Bible as though it is fact.

However, the resurrection is declared by many in the Bible. David predicted it in the Psalms. Psalm 16:10 says God would not "suffer thine Holy One (Christ) to see corruption." Job spoke of the resurrection in Job 19:25, and Isaiah predicted His resurrection in Isaiah 53. Jesus Himself predicted it many times. Matthew 16:21 says, "From that time forth began Jesus to shew unto His disciples, how that He must go unto Jerusalem, and suffer many things of the elders and chief priests and scribes, and be killed, and be raised again the third day."

Jesus says in John 2:19, "Destroy this temple (that's speaking of His body), and in three days I will raise it up." Biblical proofs of the resurrection are abundant: the empty tomb, the tremendous change in the lives of the disciples after the resurrection, and the silence of both the Romans and the Pharisees. Neither of these enemy groups ever attempted to deny Christ's resurrection. They hated it and tried to suppress it but could not refute it.

The main day of worship changed from Saturday to Sunday. The last day of the week was Saturday, the Sabbath. Jesus was resurrected on the first day of the week, Sunday, and because of His resurrection, the main day of worship was changed from Saturday to Sunday.

The existence of the church is another proof of the resurrection. The resurrection changed the disciples, and they went forth preaching Christ.

Let's look at the appearances of Christ after His resurrection, according to the Scriptural record.

His first appearance was to Mary Magdalene at the tomb after Peter and John left (John 20:11-16).

His second appearance was to the other women, who were returning from the tomb (Matthew 28:9-10).

The third was to Peter in the afternoon of the resurrection day. Significantly, Jesus went to Peter before the other disciples because of Peter's denial of Christ (Luke 24:34).

The fourth appearance was to the two as they walked on the road to Emmaus. Jesus expounded the Scriptures to them (Luke 24:13-27).

The fifth was the appearance to the disciples as the two he appeared to on the road to Emmaus were telling the disciples about their experience with Him. (Luke 24:33- 36).

His sixth appearance was to His disciples one week after His resurrection. At this time Thomas, who wasn't present when Jesus first appeared to the disciples, was there. Jesus showed him His scars and the nail holes in His hands (John 20:26-29).

Jesus said to Thomas, "Because thou hast seen Me, thou hast believed: blessed are they that have not seen, and yet have believed." I myself have not seen the risen Lord, but I believe in His bodily resurrection.

The seventh time is recorded in 1 Corinthians 15, one of the most important and crucial chapters of the Bible. This is Paul's great chapter on the resurrection, which has been given by inspiration from God. This great resurrection chapter actually deals with the Gospel. It shows that the most important part of the Gospel is the resurrection. We need to know that the resurrection was not spiritual, but it was physical. The soul never died but the body died. These bodies of ours some day will be raised (1 Corinthians 15:1-4). And I must say this: There is no Gospel — that is the good news — without the resurrection.

His eighth appearance was to some 500 people and is recounted in I Corinthians 15:6.

In verse 7 of the same chapter, the risen Lord appeared to James, the Lord's brother, Jesus' ninth appearance. There is some evidence that James was not a believer until after the resurrection. He became one of the outstanding leaders of the apostolic church.

Also verse 7 mentions that Jesus appeared to the 11 disciples. This appearance is further described in Acts 1:3-9, the time of Jesus' ascension, when he went up into Heaven from the Mount of Olives. This appearance, his 10th, was His last one to His disciples as a group.

Later the resurrected Lord appeared to Stephen just prior to his stoning in Acts 7:55-56.

Acts 9 describes Jesus' appearance to the Apostle Paul, then Saul, the persecutor of the Christian church. Saul was on the road to Damascus to get papers of authority to put believers in prison when Jesus Christ appeared to him. Paul asked who He was, and Jesus said, "I am Jesus whom thou persecutest" (Acts 9:5).

Then in Galatians 1:13-16, Jesus again appeared to Paul. This occurrence was in the Arabian desert as the Lord Jesus was teaching and grooming him to become the Apostle Paul to the Gentiles.

Later, Jesus appeared to the Apostle Paul in the temple at Jerusalem, and the Lord warned him of the persecution that was to come. This occurrence was when Jesus said He was sending Paul to the Gentiles (Acts 22:17-21). This Gospel, this good news, was going to go not to the Jews only but also to the Gentiles. Paul was going to the world, the red, yellow, black, and white. The Gospel is for whomsoever will call on the name of the Lord. This Gospel the Apostle Paul was now going to take to the Gentile nations.

Again Jesus appeared to the Apostle Paul in Acts 23:11 when he was in prison in Caesarea. The Lord stood by Paul and told him he would bear witness to Him in Rome.

The last recorded appearance of the resurrected Christ was to the Apostle John in Revelation 1:12-20. John was on the Isle of Patmos, and the Lord inspired John to write the book of Revelation.

These recorded appearances to so many people under various circumstances are proof that the resurrection of the Lord Jesus Christ is as solid as any historical fact that could be cited in the First century. It is the good news that Christ died for our sins, was buried, and rose again on the third day. He didn't vanish or disappear or stay in the grave. He rose again. The tomb is empty. Jesus Christ is alive today. These are the historical facts. This is the Gospel. The sign of Christianity is really not the Cross but the empty tomb. You can read 1 Corinthians 15 and learn more about the resurrection and what it means.

FACT 7 – Jesus is coming again.

Matthew 24:30 tells us, "And then shall appear the sign of the Son of man in Heaven (this is immediately after the Tribulation): and then shall all the tribes of the earth mourn, and they shall see the Son of man (that's Jesus) coming in the clouds of Heaven with power and great glory."

He is coming to end the Tribulation by destroying all those who have come against Jerusalem at the Battle of Armageddon. His coming will be visible. As we read in Matthew 24:17-21, He will not come as a thief in the night this time, but every eye will see Him. "For as the lightning cometh out of the east, and shineth even unto the west; so shall also the coming of the Son of Man be" (Matthew 24:27).

Lightning is very powerful and highly visible. If you close your eyes on a dark night during a thunder and lightning storm, you can still see the flashes of the lightning.

His coming will bring cataclysmic changes in the heavens. The sun will be darkened. The moon will not give light, and the stars will fall from Heaven. The entire universe will be thrown into total disarray. He is coming to judge Israel and then to judge all the nations on the earth (Matthew 25:32). At the judgment of the nations, He will separate the sheep and the goats. Not all saved people in the Tribulation will be martyred. There will be people saved during the Tribulation by the preaching of the 144,000 Jewish evangelists, who will live through the horrors of the Tribulation. These same people will have befriended the Jews and will be permitted to go into the Millennium.

Of course, we know that before His Second Coming to this earth, He is coming before the Tribulation to Rapture the church out; that is to take every living and dead believer to Heaven. His coming is the blessed hope of every believer. Titus 2:11-14 says, "For the grace of God that bringeth salvation hath appeared to all men, Teaching us that, denying ungodliness and worldly lusts, we should live soberly, righteously and godly in this present world; looking for that blessed hope, and the glorious appearing of the great God and our Savior the Lord Jesus Christ; Who gave himself for us that he might redeem us from all iniquity, and purify unto himself a peculiar people, zealous of good works."

This is the blessed hope of every believer living today. And I end with this: Even so, come quickly Lord Jesus!

CHAPTER 4 | **FACTS 22-28**

7 Facts About
The Holy Spirit

We have been talking about God the Father and God the Son. Now we are going to talk about God the Holy Spirit. The Holy Spirit has many things to do with our lives. He convicts, He convinces, He restrains, He indwells, He guides, He directs, and He draws. He is both the author of the Old Testament and the New Testament.

2 Samuel 23: 2 says, "The Spirit of the Lord spake by me, and his word was in my tongue." In 1 Corinthians 2:13 Paul says, "Not in the words which man's wisdom teacheth, but which the Holy Ghost teacheth." Peter tells us in 2 Peter 1:21, "For the Prophecy came not in old time by the will of man: but holy men of God spake as they were moved by the Holy Spirit."

Of the three basic institutions in the Bible, marriage, human government, and the local New Testament church, none is more important to the Holy Spirit than the church. The Holy Spirit was given by God the Father to the church to aid in the growth of the New Testament church period. Right now in God's program, we are in the time period of the New Testament church. This time period started when Jesus Christ was hung on the Cross of Calvary, and since that time we have been in the New Testament church era.

Remember back in the Old Testament times God chose Israel as a people for His name. They failed God, and God has sidetracked them because they rejected Jesus Christ as their Messiah. Now God has called people for His name; this group of believers is known as the church. God is now using the church, and has been using the church, since the time of the Cross to be a witness and testimony for Him to a lost and dying world. In this time of the New Testament church, the Spirit of God has been given to the church to direct, guide, appoint, anoint, and to evangelize every local New Testament church. Previously, the Holy Spirit had confined His work only to the nation of Israel. In this New Testament church era, He has come to bless all repenting sinners everywhere. His new ministry is to make all born again people like the Lord Jesus Christ.

In the Bible it is very clear that the Holy Spirit is God and that He is coexistent. He is co-eternal and co-equal with the Father and the Son. The Holy Spirit is everywhere present in the universe. He has all power. He has all knowledge. He is eternal. His name is coupled in equality with the name of the Father and the Son.

Luke 3:16 says, "John answered, saying unto them all, 'I indeed baptize you with water; but one mightier than I cometh, the latchet of whose shoes I am not worthy to unloose: he shall baptize you with the Holy Ghost and with fire.'" This is an account of John the Baptist baptizing people. John says one greater is coming than him, and His emblem in this verse is fire.

Words illustrate more about the Holy Spirit than could be put in volumes of books. Fire speaks of His consuming, purifying power in the life of all believers. We call it conviction. Have you ever been convicted by the Holy Spirit? Have you ever done something and all of a sudden something inside tells you it is wrong, don't do it? This is what we call the conviction of the Holy Spirit. This is the fire of the Holy Spirit and is a true sign of a believer. When you are convicted, you are doing wrong, according to the Bible.

In John 3:8 Jesus tells Nicodemus that the Holy Spirit is like the wind. We hear it, but we cannot tell where it comes from or where it goes. Wind speaks of His hidden depth and His mighty, regenerating power that woos a rebellious heart and convinces a sinner he needs to be saved.

In God's plan of salvation, three elements are involved in witnessing. The first element is the child of God, the second element is the Word of God, and the third element is the Holy Spirit of God. All three of these factors are involved in leading someone to the Lord Jesus Christ. As a Child of God becomes the vessel and becomes the bridge, the Word of God becomes the emphatic truth that is needed to be saved. The Spirit of God is to soften a heart to bring the person to a saving knowledge of the Lord Jesus Christ.

In John 7:37-39, Jesus refers to the Holy Spirit as water. Water speaks of His power to fill the believer to overflowing with spiritual life. Have you ever met somebody you haven't talked to about the Lord or about Christianity, but you know in your heart there is just something about them that is overflowing with joy and love? He is filled with the Spirit of God.

In Mark 1:10, the Holy Spirit's emblem is a dove. When Jesus was baptized by John, the Holy Spirit descended upon Jesus in the form of a dove. A dove speaks of His gentle, tender nature. I want to give you seven facts about the Holy Spirit.

FACT 1 – The Holy Spirit of God begins a ministry in and to the believer.

When a person gets saved, four wonderful, marvelous events occur in his or her life. The first event is a miracle takes place. Salvation is the miracle of a moment. You and I who are saved, we are miracles that God has saved us. The second wonderful event is you meet a wonderful person. You meet the Savior, the Lord Jesus Christ, the one who was seated at the right hand of God the Father, the one who left the splendors and glories of Heaven and came to this earth. "For he hath made him to be sin for us, who knew no sin; that we might be made the righteousness of God in Him" (2 Corinthians 5:21). The Son of God, He became the Son of Man, so that the sons of man might become the sons of God. You have met this wonderful person.

Number three, you become part of an eternal transaction. That word *eternal* means *forever, and ever, and ever*. It is not for a moment; it is not for a time. It is not for as long as you hold on. It is eternal. The fourth part is the Spirit of God begins a ministry in and to the believer.

FACT 2 – The Holy Spirit regenerates the believer.

He literally recreates him and gives him the nature of God. The Bible calls it a new nature. The believer becomes a new nature as Paul tells us in 2 Corinthians 5:17. God takes the believer from being a natural man (a man who has no care about the Lord, a man running away from God, who never thinks about God) to the state of being a spiritual man. The believer becomes alive in God. The believer now becomes God conscious.

FACT 3 – The Holy Spirit baptizes the believer.

1 Corinthians 12:13 says, "For by one Spirit we were all baptized into one body." The question is often asked: Does a

man have to be baptized to be saved? The answer is an emphatic *yes* but not by water baptism. Water baptism does not save you. Water baptism is an outward showing that an inward change has taken place. You need to be baptized by the Holy Spirit. He baptizes us so that all believers may be one in Christ Jesus.

This baptism is not what some people call the second baptism. A lot of people are pushing for and seeking a second baptism of the Holy Spirit, which they think makes them better than others. The second baptism of the Holy Spirit these people seek cannot be found in the Bible.

The Holy Spirit also baptizes us so that He may prepare a bride, that is the church, to be married to the Savior for all time and eternity, forever and ever. This marriage occurs after the Judgment Seat of Christ. After we are raptured off of this earth, we must appear before the Judgment Seat of Christ to give an account of the things we have done in the body. During that time, the Lord Jesus Christ is going to clean us up. The Spirit of God is going to prepare us and make us ready to become the bride of the Lord Jesus Christ. This is going to happen at the end of the seven-year Tribulation time here on earth. We (the church) are going to return with Christ (our groom). We are going to rule and reign on this earth for 1,000 years with our Lord.

FACT 4 – The Holy Spirit indwells the believer.

In 1 Corinthians 3:16 Paul says, "Know ye not that ye are the temple of God, and that the Spirit of God dwelleth in you?" In other words, He not only joins us to the Savior through baptism, but He joins Himself to us. By indwelling in us, He comes to live inside the believer's heart. His purpose is to guide and control the believer. Do you know what is exciting and marvelous about this? He will never leave you. He is with you until the day Jesus takes you home to Heaven or else raptures you off of this earth to Heaven.

FACT 5 – The Holy Spirit seals the believer.

Ephesians 4:30 says, "And grieve not the Holy Spirit of God, whereby ye are sealed unto the day of redemption." This speaks of His ownership of the believer. Once you have given your heart to Christ, once you have received Him as your personal Savior, you are not your own. You have been purchased by the precious blood of the Lord Jesus Christ. It is a transaction between you and God through Jesus Christ. The Holy Spirit seals the believer to assure him of his salvation.

Ephesians 1:13 says, "In whom ye also trusted, after that ye heard the word of truth, the gospel of your salvation: in whom also after that ye believed, ye were sealed with that Holy Spirit of promise, Which is the earnest of our inheritance until the redemption of the purchased possession, unto the praise of His glory."

Back in biblical times a father would betroth his daughter to the man she was going to marry. In the betrothal stage, the father had to put up earnest money, or a down payment, indicating that he was going to carry this through. In like manner, these verses tell us the Holy Spirit of God has become the earnest, or down payment, for our marriage to the Lord Jesus Christ. Think of it this way: The Holy Spirit is our engagement ring. When the Spirit of God seals you, He seals your name in the Book of Life. It cannot be blotted out. Revelation 21:27 states, "And there shall in no wise enter into it (Heaven) any thing that defileth, neither whatsoever worketh abomination, or maketh a lie: but they which are written in the Lamb's book of life." If you are reading this and you are saved, then the Spirit of God has sealed your name in the Book of Life. You have a home in Heaven, and no one can take that away from you.

FACT 6 – The Holy Spirit fills the believer.

Ephesians 5:18 says, "Be filled with the Spirit." This filling is different from indwelling. This filling does not mean that the believer gets more of the Holy Spirit. He is not above and beyond other believers, or a hyper spiritual person. He is not able to read Scripture and get a much more spiritual meaning out of it than you can.

When you get saved you get all of the Holy Spirit you are ever going to get. This filling is that the Holy Spirit gets more of you. John the Baptist was right when he said, "He (that's Jesus) must increase, but I must decrease" (John 3:30). God wants His influence in your life. No matter what we do or the decisions we must make, God wants to influence us. He wants His loving control over our lives. He wants our hearts. We must decrease, and He must increase. He wants us to be "…transformed by the renewing of your mind, that ye may prove what is that good, and acceptable, and perfect, will of God" (Romans 12:2). God wants to transform us to the image of Christ in our lifetime here on earth, so that we can walk even as He walked.

All six of these facts happen instantaneously. Facts 2, 3, 4, and 5 can never be lost and should never be asked for again. The sixth fact, however, can be lost, and should be asked for as many times as needed. Not too many days go by that I don't pray for the filling of the Spirit of God. Why? So that I can be emptied from carnality and sin and be filled with the Spirit. I want the words of my mouth, the meditation of my heart and the actions of my life to be acceptable in His sight to glorify my Redeemer (Psalm 19:14). Facts 2, 3, 4, and 5 give us peace with God. Fact 6 assures us of the peace of God. The sixth fact is lost whenever disobedience is found in our lives.

There are two types of disobedience. The first type is in 1 Thessalonians 5:19: "Quench not the Spirit." Thus sin involves not doing what the Holy Spirit would have us do. It is involved in witnessing. If you are witnessing to somebody and you bring them up to a point but never lead them to Christ, that is quenching the Spirit of God. Or when you are with somebody and you sense the Spirit of God telling you to witness, and you fail to do so, that is quenching the Spirit of God.

The second means of disobedience is found in Ephesians 4:30: "And grieve not the Holy Spirit of God, whereby ye are sealed until the day of redemption." This type of disobedience is doing what God does not want you to do.

FACT 7 – The Holy Spirit gives spiritual gifts.

The purpose of all spiritual gifts is to glorify the Father and to edify the church. Each believer possesses at least one spiritual gift. No believer possesses all of the spiritual gifts. There are 18 gifts mentioned in the Scriptures and are found in Romans 12, 1 Corinthians 12, and Ephesians 4.

Paul writes that he does not want us to be ignorant about spiritual gifts. Gifts fall into two categories, temporal and permanent. Paul states in 1 Corinthians 12:1 about spiritual gifts, "Now concerning spiritual gifts, brethren, I would not have you ignorant (unlearned)."

Temporal Gifts

The temporal or temporary gifts were only given for a certain time period, and then they were done away with when that period ended. This temporary time period was known as the Apostolic Church Period. This was the time after the resurrection of Christ and lasted about 100 years. During this time the Holy Spirit was directing the writing of the New Testament to holy men of God. These were mainly sign gifts and were given to authenticate and solidify, mostly to the nation of Israel, that Jesus Christ was Messiah, the King of Kings, the Lord of Lords. After the completing of the New Testament Scriptures, these gifts stopped. They were done away with; *katargeo*, it means *to stop, to cease*.

There were seven temporal gifts. One was apostleship. There are no more apostles. Although people claim to be apostles, there have been no ordained apostles since the Apostolic Church Age.

The second gift was prophecy, but there is no prophecy going on today. In other words, God has completed the Scriptures. I know people claim to be prophets, but there is no more God-given prophecy going on.

The next temporal gift is the gift of miracles. Don't get excited about this. I believe God is the God of miracles and can do miracles. There is nothing that God cannot do, and we are miracles. I have heard many accounts of miracles from missionaries and from various people who claim a miracle was performed in their lives. But people aren't going around doing miraculous things today. That gift has been done away with.

Another temporal gift is the gift of healing. Here again, don't get excited. I believe God can heal, and I know God has healed many people. I know God has healed even friends of mine, and I know that God is a healing God. But no one person has the gift of healing and can walk up to people who are laden with cancer, heart disease, ALS or any kind of tragic disease, lay their hands on them and say they are healed. I know there are people professing to be able to heal, but it is not biblical. This gift was only evident during the Apostolic Church Age when Jesus and the apostles could heal.

The fifth temporal gift was tongues, or speaking in an unknown language. Paul even says don't do this. That gift has been done away with. Here again, there are many churches that believe in this and speak in tongues, but it is not biblical. These were temporal gifts. The sixth gift was interpretation of tongues, or being able to interpret the unknown language or "tongue" spoken by another.

The seventh gift was revelatory knowledge, or the ability to receive and transmit a portion of the Word of God. This was adding new passages or books to the Bible. This gift also is done away with. We have everything God wants us to know in our Bibles.

Permanent Gifts

If you receive a gift and never unwrap it, you will never know what it is, and it will never be used. So I want you to understand these permanent gifts. Perhaps it will help you unwrap your gift(s). These gifts were given to the church for God's glory and to edify the believers. They are still in effect today.

The first permanent gift is the gift of wisdom. This is a supernatural ability to rightfully apply and employ the Word of God.

The second gift is the discerning of spirits. This is a supernatural ability to distinguish between demonic, human, and divine spirits in another person. I have heard missionaries relate accounts of this in Africa where they knew for a fact that there was a demonic spirit in the people to whom they were talking.

The third gift is the gift of giving. This is the supernatural ability to accumulate and give large amounts of one's finances to the glory of God. Many very wealthy people have given 90 percent of all they own to the Lord.

The next gift is exhortation. This gift is the supernatural ability to deliver uplifting and challenging words or encourage others with these words.

The gift of ministry is the supernatural ability to render practical help in both physical and spiritual matters.

The gift of mercy is the supernatural ability to minister to those who are in need; perhaps they are sick or afflicted.

The gift of ruling is the supernatural ability to organize, administer, and promote the various affairs in the local church.

Then there is the gift of faith. There are three kinds of biblical faith. The first kind is saving faith. The second kind is sanctifying faith. The third kind is stewardship faith, which is the supernatural ability to believe and expect great things from God, to have faith in His coming.

The gift of teaching is the supernatural ability to communicate and clarify effectively the details of the Word of God.

The gift of evangelism is the supernatural ability to lead a sinner to saving faith in Christ. All believers are not witnesses for Christ. All believers are to be witnesses for Christ, whether they have this gift or not. We who know the need are to sow the seed. Some sow the seed, some water, and some reap.

The last gift is the gift of pastor-teacher, which is the supernatural ability to preach and teach the Word of God and feed and lead the local church.

My question to you is: Are you a Spirit-controlled believer? What are your gifts? Have you unwrapped your gift, and if so, are you using it for God's purpose and glory?

CHAPTER 5 | FACTS 29-35

7 Facts About
Creation

FACT 1 – God has always existed and was the "beginner."

In Genesis 1:1 we read, "In the beginning God created the heaven and the earth." The Bible nowhere tells us where God came from. It expects us to believe that God was in the beginning and before the beginning. In fact, He was the beginner.

When God created the earth, He created time as we know it. In others words He created hours, days, weeks, months, and years. We are controlled by time. Time rules our lives. The Bible says there is a time to be born, a time to live, and a time to die. We eat at certain times, we go to bed at certain times, we have to go to work at certain times, and we work so many hours. We as human beings are bound by time. It is very hard, in fact impossible, to think back before the beginning of time when God was there. The Bible attests to the fact that God was before the beginning of time as we know it. It does not tell us where He came from but that He was at the beginning of the universe and before it.

Here are some Bible facts as to what God was doing before He created the universe. We read in John 17:5 that He was having fellowship with the son: "And now, O Father, glorify thou me with thine own self with the glory which I had with thee before the world was." John 17:24 says the Father loved the Son before the foundations of the world. Ephesians 1:4 says He was choosing the elect, "According as He hath chosen us in Him before the foundation of the world." Ephesians 3:8-9 tells us He was planning for a church. Paul was to make all men see what is the "fellowship of the mystery." The church was the mystery, "which from the beginning of the world hath been hid in God." And in Matthew 25:34, we see He was preparing for a kingdom: "Then shall the King say unto them on His right hand, Come, ye blessed of my Father, inherit the kingdom prepared for you from the foundation of the world."

1 Peter 1:18-20 says God was planning for a Savior. "Ye were not redeemed with corruptible things, as silver and gold, … But with the precious blood of Christ, as of a lamb without blemish and without spot: Who verily was foreordained before the foundation of the world." Long before He placed the first Adam in the garden, God prepared the second Adam for the Cross.

In 2 Timothy 1:9, He was developing His plan of grace: "Who hath saved us, and called us with an holy calling, not according to our works, but according to His own purpose and grace, which was given us in Christ Jesus before the world began." In Titus 1:2 He was drawing up His covenant of eternal life; "In hope of eternal life, which God, that cannot lie, promised before the world began."

FACT 2 – God created all that is, and creation reflects the triune God.

Genesis 1:1 says, "In the beginning God created…" This word *created* in Hebrew is *Exnihelo* meaning *out of nothing*. God had nothing when He created the universe and this earth. He had no blue sky, no handful of dirt, no cup of water, no seas. He had nothing. Psalms 33:6 tells us, "By the word of the Lord were the heavens made; and all the host of them by the breath of his mouth." Psalms 148:5 says, "Let them praise the name of the Lord: for He commanded, and they were created." Hebrews 11:3 tells us that the world was framed by the Word of God. Genesis 2:7 says, "And the Lord God formed man of the dust of the ground, and breathed into his nostrils the breath of life; and man became a living soul."

Jeremiah 10:12 says, "He hath made the earth by his power, he hath established the world by His wisdom, and hath stretched out the heavens by His discretion." So this created universe is really a tri-universe, reflecting the nature and personality of its triune Creator.

The universe is made up of three elements. In Genesis 1:1 we have time, space, and matter. Time has three divisions; past, present, and future. Space has three dimensions or spheres; clouds, stars, and God's abode. It also has atmosphere, ionosphere, and stratosphere. Matter is made up of three elements; energy, motion, and phenomena. The earth has a crust, a mantle, and a core. There are three basic types of energy: gravitational, electromagnetic, and nuclear. In fact, the building block of matter is the atom, and it has three parts to it — protons, neutrons, and electrons. We are trichotomous. We have a body, soul, and spirit. I could go on and on about this. God has made His creation to reflect Himself; this created universe reveals the trinity of God.

Psalms 118:23 states, "This is the Lord's doing; it is marvellous in our eyes." The natural world has been very carefully located with precision in our solar system. It has been meticulously planned by God. Its structures are highly ordered, and its processes precisely controlled.

FACT 3 – The Theory of Evolution does not hold up to scrutiny.

Theory is speculative. It is a supposition. It is not 100 percent proven. On the other hand, a fact is something that is true. Evolution's god is the awesome force of nature that supposedly drives all life forward in gradual steps of progress. It's called uniformitarianism, which states that during millions of years, things evolved from simple forms into their present state. The evolutionist needs time on his side. The Theory of Evolution forms a basis of secular humanism or survival of the fittest, situation ethics, and a morality based on a moment. "If it feels good, do it." Evolution is the speculative theory of life and the universe starting without God.

The modern scientific and educational establishments are almost entirely committed to total evolutionism. They maintain that the physical universe evolved from nothing at all but a primeval particle that rapidly inflated and then exploded into the so-called Big Bang Theory. From this, the universe has been rapidly expanding ever since, somehow enabling planets, stars, and galaxies to form. On earth there was a one-cell organism that was fused in mud. A transformation occurred, and by evolution a tadpole was formed. And then it turned into a fish and then into a shark, and over millions of years, the shark was washed up on a beach. The shark lay there for another million years, and it finally realized that it had grown legs and arms. Through environmental adaptation, it got up and began to walk. One day it walked into the jungle, and again after millions of years, it evolved into an anthropoid or simian. An ape or a monkey roamed the jungle for millions of years and eventually evolved into the primeval ape man or cave man. After another few million years of evolution, we finally got man as we are today.

As an intelligent, thinking person, how does this scenario sound? Pretty off the wall, isn't it? Believe it or not, this idea is what is essentially taught as absolute fact in practically every school in the Western world from the elementary grades through graduate school. It also dominates the news media and our television shows such as *Nova* and *National Geographic*. The theory has even infiltrated into our legal and political systems.

How did evolution come about?

The great divide between those who believe in biblical creation and those who don't has existed for centuries. As early as the 6th century B.C., some Greeks denied creationism or intelligent design. They believed life originated under water and began spontaneously. Others believed men developed by gradual stages from fish. In the 1st century, the Apostle Paul confronted the philosophers of Athens by referring to God who made the world and everything that is in it (Acts 17:24). Here Paul is giving a biblical testimony to the creative act of God.

Evolution can best be traced to Charles Darwin, who is known as the father of the modern evolutionary theory. Charles Darwin was born in Shrewsbury, England, in 1809. As a boy he had a keen interest in nature and science. His father was a physician. At his father's urging, he studied medicine at the University of Edinburg but did not like it. After two years, he transferred to Christ's College in Cambridge for theological studies. He wrote, "I did not then in the least doubt the strict and literal truth of every word in the Bible."

After graduating from Christ's College, he briefly considered becoming a minister; however, in 1831 he signed up to serve on a British science expedition aboard the *HMS Beagle* for a five-year voyage. The ship sailed down to South America and to the Galapagos Islands off the coast of Ecuador in the Pacific Ocean. As the ship would make stops along the way, Darwin would go on shore and collect plants, animals, and fossils. He came to the conclusion that species thrived and adapted to circumstances by some sort of biological mechanism. They evolved and adapted to their environment by random chance that favored them with traits that allowed them to flourish in their environment.

After some 20 years of analysis and research, in 1859, he published his conclusions and theory in a book called *The Origin of Species*. Darwin was somewhat reluctant to print this book. He knew it would arouse the wrath of millions who believed in biblical creation. He once told a friend, "This book is like confessing to a murder." His book was immediately accepted and was recognized by eminent scientists, philosophers, and liberal theologians as a piece of ground-breaking work.

Darwin said, "I never gave up Christianity until I was 40 years of age." He later wrote in 1880, "I am sorry to have to inform you that I do not believe in the Bible as a divine revelation and therefore not in Jesus Christ as the Son of God." Darwin had become a self-proclaimed agnostic. An agnostic says it is impossible to know whether God exists. Darwin died in 1882 without Christ.

Evolution runs contrary to the Second Law of Thermodynamics, which describes the universe as a wound-up clock that is slowly running down. It is also known as the Law of Decay. Evolution has all life being built up from simpler forms to more complex forms. The Book of Genesis informs us life began on dry land, while evolution says it originated in some slimy sea. Evolutionists have Adam evolving from an ape. In Genesis he was originally and suddenly made in the very image of God.

The whole enterprise of science is to explain life without invoking supernatural explanations. The evolutionists say intelligent design is not science. It is a religion, and it should not be taught in a science classroom. Evolution has become so deeply ingrained in public education that it is being taught as fact or the gospel truth instead of a theory devised by mortal man. Evolution has never been observed — basic plant and animal life has not changed over the years. However, the earth can be observed to be round by our astronauts as they look down at the earth from space. Or if you look at an eclipse, you can see the roundness of the earth as it passes through the moon, and this is all based on biblical fact. An evolutionist can observe the present state of the universe, but he or she must speculate about its beginning and history.

Satan's plan is quite ingenious. He has found a way to convince humanity that people are the product of an impersonal and voluntary, or evolutionary, force and that they are therefore not responsible to any divine being. The fight is not merely about origins, but it is about destinies.

FACT 4 – Creation versus evolution.

The world that exists was formed by the Word of God as stated in Hebrews 11:3. This complex, highly energized universe could never in all eternity have evolved by the collision of two asteroids — an idea promoted by the evolutionists — known as the Big Bang Theory, which they say occurred some 13.7 billion years ago. Nor could life have begun in these complex, wonderful bodies that we have by evolving from a tadpole in a warm mud puddle.

Genesis 1:27 says, "God created man in His own image, in the image of God created He him; male and female, created He them." Consider this world we live in. It is:

- Orbiting around the sun some 584,000,000 miles in one solar year;
- Keeping its constant distance of 93 million miles from the sun;
- Revolving on its axis one complete revolution every 24 hours bringing us night and day;
- Keeping its balance and alignment with the sun and its equatorial location (the line of the equator).

Then consider its axle inclination as it tilts 23 degrees 44 minutes toward the sun and again tilts 23 degrees 44 minutes away from the sun, which provides the summer and winter solstice, and our summer and fall equinox, which in turn gives us our seasons of spring, summer, fall, and winter. In addition, consider the rain, the hydrological functions of the earth as the heat of the sun's rays on the waters of the ocean draws moisture up into the air, and clouds are formed. From this sea-drawing action, air currents are produced and drive these clouds toward a cooler climate, which is produced over the land mass. When these clouds of moisture come over the cool land mass, a process known as condensation occurs, which turns warm moisture into droplets of water, which in turn, by the gravitational force of the earth, pulls these water droplets to the earth. The vegetation of the earth is watered, which supports growth, and then the excess waters run into the streams and rivers and continue to the ocean. This drainage of water occurs because of the topography of the earth that God brought forth through the flood.

Job 36:27-28 says, "For He maketh small the drops of water: they pour down rain according to the vapour thereof: Which the clouds do drop and distil upon man abundantly." Ecclesiastes 1:7 says, "All the rivers run into the sea; yet the sea is not full; unto the place from whence the rivers come, thither they return again."

Consider the balance of the earth, of the waters and the vast land mass as it rotates on its axis some 1,100 miles per hour, and it does not wobble. We don't even know that we are spinning that fast on the earth's axis.

It is illogical and absurd to think and believe this complex universe we live in could have started by chance and randomly happened without any intelligence being behind it. The boundless space, the endless time, the infinite energy and the innumerable complexities of the universe all unite in an irrefutable testimony to the God of all creation. It is intellectually prudent to understand and believe this universe did not come into existence through evolution. We live in a very ordered and balanced universe controlled only by its Creator, who spoke it into existence spontaneously in a moment of time.

In God's conversation with Job and his friends in Job 38:4, God says, "Where wast thou when I laid the foundations of the earth?" I believe God because He was there, and I was not. Although God's creation of the heavens and the earth is winding down, and this creation is now groaning in pain under the effects of sin and the curse, there is a glorious future waiting for the redeemed. Those of us who are saved when the Lord returns He will deliver from corruption. Isaiah 65:17 says, "For, behold, I create new heavens and a new earth: and the former shall not be remembered, nor come into mind." Isaiah 66:22 says, "For as the new heavens and the new earth, which I will make, shall remain before me, saith the Lord."

2 Peter 3:13 tells us, "Nevertheless we, according to his promise, look for new heavens and a new earth, wherein dwelleth righteousness." Not only will no sin be present there, neither will the results of sin and the curse be present there. Revelation 21:1-4 states, "And I saw a new Heaven and a new earth: for the first Heaven and the first earth were passed away ... And God shall wipe away all tears from their eyes; and there shall be no more death, neither sorrow, nor crying, neither shall there be any more pain: for the former things are passed away."

Aren't these Bible verses marvelous!

FACT 5 – The Biblical fact of Genesis 1:1 and 1:2.

In Genesis 1:1-2, God told us what He did. In the next verses of this chapter, He told us how He did it, how He put it all together. The first chapter of Genesis is and has been one of great controversy. On the one hand you have the evolutionists saying this chapter is not true, and on the other hand, you have the special creationists (believers) saying every word of this chapter is true (plenary verbal inspiration). All the Word of God is true.

The evolutionists say that between Genesis 1:1 and Genesis 1:3 there was a gap of time. This is known as the Gap Theory. It states that billions of years elapsed between verses 1 and 3, and it is largely based on the fossils of plants and animals found in the earth's fossiliferous stratus. They claim these organisms died millions of years ago. This theory faces a real problem in the New Testament. Paul states in Romans 5:12 that man's (Adam's) sin brought about the death of all things on the earth. Man, plants, and animals on this earth did not die until Adam sinned, and that sin did not happen until Genesis 3.

Exodus 20:11, part of the Ten Commandments, states in six days the Lord made Heaven and earth. Thus, nothing on the earth or sea could have been made before the six days of creation. The Gap Theory was accepted by Bible theologians as they compromised the Word of God for an unbelieving scientific community.

The events of the six days of creation took place before there were any human beings to observe and record them. They would have to be revealed by God either to Moses or more likely originally to Adam himself. Genesis 1 and 2 say the universe was created by an intelligent designer — far, far, far above our intelligence.

I am an architect. My profession is design. I have been designing for 40 years. I have designed hundreds of buildings. I live design. I sleep design. I think design. There is one crucial rule of design every good designer adheres to and that is form follows function. Let me explain this to you.

If you were a client of mine and you came to my office and wanted me to design a house for you, I would not go to a drawer and pull out a pretty picture and say, "Here is your house." How would you know what is in the house? You are coming to me with a wish list that has everything you would like to have in the house. What I would have to do is take your wish list and functionalize the house. In other words, put everything in order and make all the spaces function according to other spaces so that there is a proper and logical circulation plan done according to the functions of the house. When I showed you the picture of the house, I was getting the form ahead of the function. I did not functionalize (plan) your house according to your wish list.

After the function of your house is complete, I will then put the form to it. The form is the way your house looks from the outside (it's the visual image). It consists of the materials I chose to use (i.e. stone, brick, etc.), the size of windows and their placement, the style of roof, the scale and proportion of the various exterior elements, and other details to give your house an aesthetically, pleasing look and form in the architectural style you want.

The evolutionists say that according to Genesis 1:2, there was no form on the earth. It was void, and the earth lay this way for millions — and maybe billions — of years.

What the greatest and most intelligent designer (who is God) was doing through the Spirit of God as He moved over the waters in verse 2 was giving it its gravitational force field. The Spirit of God was giving it its electromagnetic field. He was starting the earth's rotation on its axis. He was starting its solar orbit. He was functionalizing the earth, so He could now put form to it. He could now put the land mass, the oceans, and the mountains in a logical order. As the most intelligent designer, He was following that rule. In fact, He created the rule that form follows function. This is the most intelligent way design works.

FACT 6 – The age of the earth.

Evolutionists tell us the earth is 13.7 billion years old, but the Bible gives us a clear indication of how old the earth is. From creation to the flood was 1,656 years. From the flood to the call of Abraham was 367 years, and from Abraham to the birth of Christ was 2,000 years. From the death of Christ to this present day a little more than 2,000 years have passed. If you add up these years, you get between 6,035 years and 6,070 years.

There was an experiment conducted known as the RATE Data. It was conducted by Dr. Russell Humphreys. He tested the helium and rock crystals and how long it takes helium to escape from radioactive crystals. This new experiment supports the age of the earth to be approximately 6,000 years.

FACT 7 – Man is the height of God's creation.

Man was the highlight of God's creation. Man was absolutely unique. He was made in the image of God. He was declared king of creation. He was commanded to obey God. He was encouraged to eat of all of the other trees in the garden. He was given a wife.

Only men and women were created in the image of God. Obviously men and women play a vital part in God's wonderful plan for this earth. God has entrusted them, or entrusted us, with stewardship over the earth and its animal inhabitants. This privilege has been called the dominion mandate of Genesis 1:28. It entails great responsibility.

The dominion applies only to the earth. There are innumerable stars and galaxies in the heavens. In the ages to come, the dominion mandate may be extended to cover the entire universe, and we who have accepted the Lord Jesus Christ as our Savior may be assigned that dominion to explore and develop for the glory of our God. What exciting service to render throughout eternity to our Master and our Lord!

Man was the highlight of all of God's creation. We are the reason behind this magnificent universe and this marvelous earth we inhabit. Psalm 139:14 says we are "fearfully and wonderfully made." When you sense any of earth's phenomena, know this: God made it just for you. We are ordinary people chosen for a truly extraordinary future in eternity to come.

CHAPTER 6 | FACTS 36-42

7 Facts About
Sin

Denying the existence and presence of sin is impossible. If sin were not a fact, there would be no crime, no jails, no prisons, no locks on doors, and no police forces and so on. Sin is universal. Everybody is involved in it. 1 Kings 8:46 says, "For there is no man that sinneth not." Ecclesiastes 7:20 says, "For there is not a just man upon the earth, that doeth good and sinneth not." I would like to give you seven facts about sin. When I began my study on sin, the first two facts were very startling to me.

FACT 1 – Man makes so little of sin.

Man denies sin. He makes light of it. He jokes about it. He says it is the invention of some religious fanatic. To some, sin is the weakness of the flesh, and to others, it is the absence of good. To the so-called scholar, it is ignorance. To the evolutionist and atheist, it is the nature of the beasts. To the humanist, it is a disease and needs to be treated by science. To some, sin is relative or in other words, "If it feels good, do it." To the "Now Generation," it is being politically correct. You cannot be intolerant of sin.

Yesterday's immoralities have become today's moralities. Yesterday's unacceptable standards have become today's acceptable standards. There is no care or concern about sin. Immorality is at an all-time high. The world is in a moral decline.

FACT 2 – God makes so much of sin.

Sin is an abomination unto God. He hates sin. It is unlawful. He can't stand sin. Sin is disgusting to Him. He shudders at it. He detests sin. He turns away from it. Sin grieves the heart of Almighty God. By actual count, sin is referred to more than 700 times in the Word of God. God gives people who live in sin over to a reprobate mind.

When you think of sin, you think of a number of words such as *iniquity*. Iniquity is *lawlessness, wickedness, unrighteousness, wrong-doing, evil-doing*. Two words in the Greek New Testament define sin. *Hamartia* is *to miss the mark*. I call it moral obliquity. The other word, *parabasis,* is *transgression or to overstep a forbidden line or to trespass*. You can do this deliberately or accidentally. For instance, if you are walking in the mountain and you come to a posted sign that says "No trespassing," that means you are not supposed to step over that line and go on the other person's land. He doesn't want you there. Another case is you are walking in the mountain and all of a sudden you turn around and see a sign that says "No trespassing." You were on that person's property accidentally. You were unaware of the trespass notices. This is *parabasis*.

FACT 3 – Sin is defined very clearly in the Bible.

1 John 3:4 says, "Sin is the transgression of the law." In other words when you transgress, you trespass the law of God. That

would be the Ten Commandments. In fact, sin could be held to even our secular laws. For instance, if the speed limit is 55 miles per hour, and you go 70 miles per hour, you are trespassing against the law. You are deliberately speeding; That could be counted as sin in the eyes of God. You are not being obedient to the laws of the land. This is *parabasis* or *overstepping*.

Romans 3:23 says sin is coming short of God's glory. This is *hamartia* or *missing the mark*. 1 John 5:10 says unbelief is sin and makes God a liar. 1 John 5:17 says all unrighteousness is sin. In Isaiah 1, sin is rebellion against God. In Isaiah 53:6, sin is going your own way, planning your own life according to your own will, without seeking the will of God. Sin is falling short of God's purpose for your life. Sin is assuming independence from God by departing from His will.

Sin can be summarized as threefold:
1. It is an act of direct disobedience to the revealed will of God.
2. It is a state in which there is an absence of righteousness.
3. It is a nature or enmity toward God (hatred). Many humanists and atheists are like this and don't believe in God and hate God.

How did sin get here? The next fact will help answer this.

FACT 4 – The Bible tells us about the origin of sin.

Ezekiel 28 and Isaiah 14 tell us sin began with the anointed cherub named Lucifer. He was an angel that was tired of being an angel and wanted to be God. He very brazenly one day walked into the throne room of God and told God his five deadly "I wills." In other words, he was saying, "God, I am moving in, and You are moving out." Then he led a rebellion against God. For that, God cast him out of Heaven along with one-third of the angels that joined him in his rebellion; they became demons. He then moved into the human arena and introduced into the universe a new evil element hitherto unknown; this perverted element was sin.

Sin entered the world in Genesis 3. It says, "And the Lord God commanded the man, saying, Of every tree of the garden thou mayest freely eat: But of the tree of the knowledge of good and evil, thou shalt not eat of it: for in the day thou eatest thereof thou shalt surely die." What God was doing here was giving His first created man, Adam, a commandment. "You may eat of all the trees but one. Don't eat of the Tree of Knowledge." The consequence was if he ate of this tree, he would surely die.

In Genesis 3:1 we read, "Now the serpent was more subtil than any beast of the field which the Lord God had made. And he said unto the woman, 'Yea, hath God said, Ye shall not eat of every tree of the garden?'" What Satan was doing here and what he is doing today is saying, "Are you sure God said this? Are you sure this is God's way? Are you sure the Bible is true?" He is putting doubt into a person's mind about God and His Word.

Genesis 3:4 says, "And the serpent said unto the woman, Ye shall not surely die." Satan was actually calling God a liar. Verse 6 says, "And when the woman saw that the tree was good for food, and that it was pleasant to the eyes, and a tree to be desired to make one wise, she took of the fruit thereof, and did eat, and gave also unto her husband with her; and he did eat." Adam and Eve were in direct disobedience to the will of God.

Sin entered the world when the will of God was resisted, the word of God was rejected, and the way of God was deserted. According to Ephesians 2:2, Satan's domain is the air around the earth, and he walks up and down the highways and byways of this earth like a roaring lion seeking whom he may devour. He is continually trying to get as many people as he can to join in his rebellion against God, for he is God's archenemy.

FACT 5 – Sin is natural.

Romans 5:12 tells us, "Wherefore, as by one man sin entered into the world, and death by sin; and so death passed upon all men, for that all have sinned." This means death has passed upon everybody who has been conceived on this earth.

God placed sin on the whole human race because of Adam's actions in the garden. Adam was representing the whole human race, and God took the sin of Adam and placed it to our account. We are born sinners. People don't have to be taught to sin. We are sinners because we sin, and we sin because we are sinners.

Romans 3:23 says, "For all have sinned, and come short of the glory of God." We sin by choice because we are sinners by nature, so sin is natural. It is doing what comes naturally. This is why God separates the natural man from the spiritual man. The natural man receiveth not the things of God. They are spiritually unconcerned about what God has to say.

The Apostle Paul writes about sin and our sin nature in Romans 7:18-19: "For I know that in me (that is in my flesh,) dwelleth no good thing: for to will is present with me; but how to perform that which is good I find not. For the good that I would I do not: but the evil which I would not, that I do."

Sin takes you farther than you want to go, sin keeps you longer than you want to stay, and sin always costs you more than you want to pay.

FACT 6 – Sin has its consequences.

Sin has immediate consequence. Lucifer lost his coveted position as Heaven's anointed cherub as he became earth's depraved dragon. His future consequence is to be cast into the lake of fire where he will be forever and ever (Revelation 20:10).

Romans 6:23 says, "For the wages of sin is death." As a result of man's sin, there are two deaths. There is a physical death and a spiritual death. Death does not annihilate one or cease one from being. Death only separates. It separates the soul and spirit from the body. This is a physical death. This is what Adam experienced in Genesis 5:5. He died because of sin, and every human being since then, except for two, Enoch and Elijah, has experienced death. If Jesus tarries, we are going to experience death. This is because of sin.

Sin separates you from God. This is a spiritual separation. Natural men, those who do not receive Christ as their Savior, are separated from God. 2 Thessalonians 1:7-8 says, "And to you who are troubled rest with us, when the Lord Jesus shall be revealed from Heaven with His mighty angels, In flaming fire taking vengeance on them that know not God, and that obey not the Gospel of our Lord Jesus Christ: Who shall be punished with everlasting destruction from the presence of the Lord, and from the glory of His power."

It will separate the unsaved person from the mercy of God forever. This is eternal separation. Revelation 20:6 says, "Blessed and holy is he that hath part in the first resurrection: on such the second death hath no power, but they shall be priests of God and of Christ, and shall reign with Him a thousand years." Revelation 21:8 says, "But the fearful and unbelieving, and the abominable, and murderers, and whoremongers, and sorcerers, and idolaters, and all liars, shall have their part in the lake which burneth with fire and brimstone: which is the second death."

Again in Revelation 20:15 it says, "And whosoever was not found written in the book of life was cast into the lake of fire." Revelation 21:27 says, "And there shall in no wise enter into it any thing that defileth, neither whatsoever worketh abomination, or maketh a lie: but they which are written in the Lamb's book of life." This spiritual death is eternal separation from God and His mercy forever.

Let us consider some of the various kinds of sin as indicated in the Bible. There is a sin of ignorance. Jesus said, "Father, forgive them; for they know not what they do" (Luke 23:34). Sometimes people do things, and they don't realize that it is sin they are committing against God.

Then there is sin of infirmity or moral weakness. "Who can understand the error of his way? Psalm 19:12 says, "Cleanse thou me from secrets faults." There are sins of carelessness. Psalm 39:1 says, "I said, I will take heed to my ways, that I sin not with my tongue."

Then there are sins of presumption, which is when you take things for granted. Psalm 19:13 tells us, "Keep back thy servant also from presumptuous sins." Then there is the unpardonable sin, which is the sin of rejecting the Holy Spirit for salvation. God can forgive all sin but the rejection of Christ as Savior. If the Spirit of God touches somebody's heart to receive Christ and they continue to reject, God will turn them over to a reprobate heart or mind. They are hopelessly sinful and will never receive Christ. Their choice is to not receive Christ as their Savior, and they commit the unpardonable sin. God cannot pardon them from this sin.

Then there is the sin unto death. 1 Corinthians 11:30 says, "For this cause many are weak and sickly among you, and many sleep." This sin can only be committed by believers. It happens when the believer lives such a wretched life that the Father finally reaches down and takes him home to Heaven earlier than he normally would have.

These verses in 1 Corinthians 11 are talking about communion that you take at church. When you take the cup, which represents the blood, and the bread, which represents the broken body of Christ, the Bible tells us to examine ourselves before we partake of it. Before you take communion, you should examine yourself and go through your mind and heart and be confessed up to date because you do not want to take that bread and cup unworthily. The Bible says some are weak, some are sickly and many sleep. In other words, many die before their time because they took communion in an unworthy manner.

Sin dulls man's ear, it darkens his understanding, it diverts his feet, it defiles his tongue, it deceives his heart, it devours his intellect, and it dooms his soul. Being a Christian does not exempt or isolate you from sinning. The preventative against sin is the Word of God. Psalm 119:11 notes, "Thy word have I hid in mine heart, that I might not sin against Thee." In other words if you know the Word of God and have memorized the Word of God, you are less likely to sin. The Bible says we are not ignorant of Satan's temptations against us. Every one of us has different temptations. When Satan's demons are tempting you to disobey God, if you use the Word of God and have Satan get behind you, Satan will flee from you. The Lord Jesus Christ did that. He used the Word of God in those instances when He was being tempted, and the Bible says the devil left Him (Matthew 4:1-11). I tell you from experience that the devil will leave you if you use the Word of God. It will defeat him.

Also, if you allow God to have His way and influence over your life, you are living a spirit-controlled life. This is a life that is being filled by the Spirit of God daily, so you can walk in the Spirit. There is also a desire or determination to be holy as He is holy. These are all preventative methods to be used against sin when you are being buffeted or tempted by Satan himself and his demons.

FACT 7 – Thanks be to God that He has a remedy for sin for the Christian and for the non-Christian.

Romans 6:12 says, "Let not sin therefore reign in your mortal body, that ye should obey it in the lust thereof." Romans 6:14 says, "For sin shall not have dominion over you: for ye are not under the law, but under grace." In Romans 6:1 Paul says, "What shall we say then? Shall we continue in sin, that grace may abound?" In Romans 6:2 Paul says, "God forbid."

Paul writes in Romans 7:24-25, "O wretched man that I am! who shall deliver me from the body of this death? I thank God through Jesus Christ our Lord. So then with the mind I myself serve the law of God; but with the flesh the law of sin." Paul was thanking God that through the Lord Jesus Christ he can be delivered from sin.

Romans 3:25 says, "Whom God hath set forth to be a propitiation through faith in his blood." We read in 1 John 2:2, "And he is the propitiation for our sins: and not for ours only, but also for the sins of the whole world." I John 4:10 tells us, "Herein is love, not that we loved God, but that He loved us, and sent his Son to be the propitiation for our sins." Too much emphasis cannot be placed on the fact that Christ is the propitiation for our sin. In other words, Christ is the acceptable sacrifice for our sins.

Only through Jesus Christ can one have his or her sins forgiven. "For God sent not his Son into the world to condemn the world; but that the world through Him might be saved" (John 3:17). Christ came into the world to save sinners. Christ was the promised redeemer of Genesis 3:15. After Adam and Eve sinned in the garden, God got Adam, Eve, and the serpent together and explained to them that someday he was going to send a Redeemer. He was promising that a Redeemer would come to save them from their sin. 1 Peter 1:18-19 says, "You were not redeemed with corruptible things, as silver and gold … But with the precious blood of Christ, as of a lamb without blemish and without spot."

"But God commendeth his love toward us, in that, while we were yet sinners, Christ died for us" (Romans 5:8). He who knew no sin was made sin for us "that we might be made the righteousness of God in Him" (2 Corinthians 5:21). Isaiah 53:4 tells us that our sins were laid on Him. He bore our sins in His own body on the Cross (1 Peter 2:24). And with His stripes, we are healed of sin (Isaiah 53:5).

For there is no other name under Heaven whereby a man can be saved (Acts 4:12). "That if thou shalt confess with thy mouth the Lord Jesus, and shalt believe in thine heart that God hath raised Him from the dead, thou shalt be saved" (Romans 10:9-10). "For whosoever shall call upon the name of the Lord shall be saved" (Romans 10:13). "As far as the east is from the west, so far hath he removed our transgressions from us" (Psalm 103:12). "Though your sins be as scarlet, they shall be as wool" (Isaiah 1:18).

Isaiah 38:17 tells us God has cast our sins behind His back, and He remembers them no more. Hebrews 8:12 says, "For I will be merciful to their unrighteousness, and their sins and their iniquities will I remember no more." "If we confess our sins, he is faithful and just to forgive us our sins, and to cleanse us from all unrighteousness" (1 John 1:9).

God's remedy is greater than all of our sins and much broader than the scope of our transgressions. It is the marvelous grace of our Living Lord, grace that exceeds our sins and our guilt, yonder on Calvary's mount outpoured, there where the blood of the Lamb was spilled. It is His grace that will pardon and cleanse within, grace that is greater than all of our sin.

CHAPTER 7 | FACTS 43-49

7 Facts About
Salvation

Salvation is the most dynamic word in the English language. Today we are living in a pluralistic society. *Pluralism* is defined as *all religions are equal*. They have different views, but all views are right. You will obtain salvation some way and go to Heaven no matter what religion you follow. The word *salvation* means *to affect successfully the full delivery of someone or something from impending danger*. The very word carries with it the implication that someone or something needs to be saved and that someone is able and willing to save.

To experience salvation according to the Bible, you need to be converted. Acts 3:19 says, "Repent ye therefore, and be converted." The word *converted* has reference to a twofold turning on the part of an individual. One has to do with *repentance*, which is a *turning from*, and the other has to do with *faith*, which is a *turning to*. Acts 20:21 says, "Repentance toward God, and faith toward our

Lord Jesus Christ." So repentance is not reforming. It is a voluntary and sincere change in the mind of the sinner causing him to turn from sin. The sin that would condemn a person to hell is the sin of rejecting the Lord Jesus Christ as their personal Savior.

The second part of conversion is faith. Faith is not a feeling nor is it an opinion. Faith is a voluntary and sincere change in the mind of the sinner causing him to turn to the Savior and accept the Lord Jesus Christ in his heart. I want to give you seven biblical facts about salvation.

FACT 1 – Salvation was God's plan from the beginning.

Do you think God did not know about Adam and Eve's actions in the garden? He foreknew that Adam and Eve would eat of the tree of which He had told them not to eat. He is omniscient, which is one of His attributes. He knows all things even before they occur. The plan of salvation was drawn up by God before Genesis 1:1, before the foundations of the world were ever laid.

Seven things God was doing before He created the universe:
1. He was having fellowship with the Son.
2. He was choosing the elect.
3. In Ephesians 3:8-9, He was planning for a church. Paul was to make all men see what is the fellowship of the mystery. The church was the mystery, which from the beginning of the ages has been hidden in God, who has created all things by Jesus Christ.
4. He was preparing for a kingdom.
5. He was developing His plan of grace instead of works for salvation, "According to his own purpose and grace, which was given us in Christ Jesus before the world began" (2 Timothy 1:9).
6. He was drawing up His covenant of eternal life. Titus 1:2 tells us, "In hope of eternal life, which God, that cannot

lie, promised before the world began." God knew about our sin nature before the foundations of the world and that the Lamb, Jesus Christ, would need to be slain.

7. He was planning for a Savior. 1 Peter 1:18-20 says, "Ye were not redeemed with corruptible things, as silver and gold … But with the precious blood of Christ, as of a lamb without blemish and without spot. Who verily (truly) was foreordained before the foundations of the world." Long before He placed the first Adam in the garden, God prepared the second Adam for the Cross. God, in his foreknowledge, knew the man and woman He made and put in the garden and gave them the option of choice. He knew they would choose poorly. Sin did not take God by surprise. Therefore, the triune God formed this marvelous plan of salvation involving the Lord Jesus Christ and the Holy Spirit.

FACT 2 – Salvation is a must.

Salvation is imperative. Many people have had a moral reformation but never a Messiah regeneration. In John 3 when Nicodemus asked Jesus how to get to Heaven, His answer was "Except a man be born again, he cannot see the kingdom of God. … Ye must be born again." There are no exceptions. Pluralism is not going to result in salvation. Literally billions of people living on this God-created earth, believe the imperative of salvation doesn't matter. The devil has them so entangled in the things of this world; they have no care or concern about life after death.

Know this: God continues to pursue mankind. He implores them. He begs them. He pleads with all humanity to accept His marvelous plan of salvation. God is long-suffering. 1 Peter 1:23 says, "Being born again, not of corruptible seed, but of incorruptible, by the Word of God, which liveth and abideth for ever." We have been redeemed by the incorruptible blood of Christ to an incorruptible inheritance, an incorruptible body, and an incorruptible crown to serve an incorruptible King all revealed and activated through the incorruptible eternal Word of God.

Being born again is not by water, which is a physical birth, but by the Word of God, which is a spiritual birth. Romans 10:17 says, "So then faith cometh by hearing, and hearing by the word of God." The Greek word for born again is *Palingenesia*. *Pali* means *again*, and *genesia* means *birth*. Salvation is a new birth and a new life in Christ.

FACT 3 – Salvation is by grace alone.

God has dealt with people in different time periods in the Old and New Testaments, but He saves them all in the same threefold way.

1. Salvation is always by blood. Hebrews 9:22 says, "Without shedding of blood is no remission."
2. Salvation is always through a person. 1 Thessalonians 5:9 says, "For God hath not appointed us to wrath, but to obtain salvation by our Lord Jesus Christ."
3. Salvation can only be had through grace. Ephesians 2:8-9 says, "For by grace are ye saved through faith; and that not of yourselves: it is the gift of God: Not of works, lest any man should boast."

John 3:16 says, "For God so loved the world, that He gave his only begotten Son, that whosoever believeth in him should not perish, but have everlasting life." The devil has twisted, turned, stretched, reversed, and hidden this passage from millions of people. Most people you talk with about salvation and Heaven and how they can get there are working their way to Heaven. They say and believe it is by works of righteousness that they have done. This is opinion versus knowledge. I am trying to give you Bible knowledge, so you can give biblical facts to people when they come up with their own opinions about the Bible.

Most churches teach that you are saved by works. Here are seven of the works they condone:
1. Belonging to a church and having church membership.
2. Being baptized as a baby.
3. Being a good, moral person, in other words, trying to keep all of the Ten Commandments.
4. Loving and tolerating everyone.
5. Giving money to the church.
6. Attending church on Sunday.
7. Coming from a Christian family and living in a Christian country.

Grace and mercy are two of the outstanding characteristics of God. Grace is defined as getting something we do not deserve. Mercy is defined as not getting what we do deserve. Grace and mercy are interconnected or coupled together with salvation. They are the foundation of salvation. His grace is greater than all of our sin and broader than the scope of our transgressions.

FACT 4 – Biblical salvation is the only way to eternal life.

An old spiritual song has the phrase "Everybody talking about Heaven ain't going there." Jesus said in John 14:6, "I am the way, the truth, and the life: no man cometh unto the Father, but by me."

Peter told the Sanhedrin in Acts 4:12, "Neither is there salvation in any other: for there is none other name under heaven given among men, whereby we must be saved." These are days of great deception. There seems to be little question that the age in which we live is rapidly drawing to a close. This being true, the devil is multiplying his efforts to deceive and to mislead people to counterfeit systems.

One of the devil's sharpest controls is counterfeit religion. Contrary to what many believe, the devil's main strategy is by way of imitation or fraudulent belief. The devil is able to ensnare the unwary and ignorant into the pits of eternal death. Instead of fighting the church on the outside like he did during the rule of Rome when Rome outwardly persecuted the Christians, the devil moved inside the church. He is now fighting the battle from the inside. Instead of being saved by grace, many believe they can be saved by works.

The devil is not opposed to the dishonest use of Scripture. In fact, this is one of his most treacherous tools, knowing that men and women probably will not respond to a religion wholly given over to his worship. He cunningly and insidiously seeks to make his false system resemble the genuine and his doctrine to sound as if it is the very truth of God. Most of the false cults of today abound in quotations and misquotations from the Bible. You will never find these false systems teaching or believing in the death of Christ on the Cross and His sacrificial blood as the payment for our sin.

1 Timothy 4:1 says, "Now the Spirit speaketh expressly, that in the latter times some shall depart from the faith, giving heed to seducing spirits, and doctrines of demons." 2 Corinthians 4:4 says, "In whom the god of this world (that is Satan) hath blinded the minds of them which believe not." Biblical salvation is the only way to Heaven and eternal life. More than 100 times, the New Testament urges the sinner to believe in Christ, to receive Him, to trust Him, to depend upon Him. When this is sincerely done, complete pardon from sin and all of the benefits of salvation are immediately received.

FACT 5 – Salvation is for everyone.

God has no pleasure in the death of the wicked, the unsaved. 1 Timothy 2:4 says, "Who will have all men to be saved, and to come unto the knowledge of the truth." When a person accepts Christ as his or her personal Savior, God places the righteousness of the Lord Jesus Christ to that person's account.

Romans 3:22 tells us the righteousness of God is for everyone, but it only comes to rest on those who believe." Romans 5:8 says, "But God commendeth his love toward us, in that, while we were yet sinners, Christ died for us." Acts 17:30 says God "commandeth all men every where to repent." Acts 20:21 says, "Testifying both to the Jews and also to the Greeks, repentance toward God, and faith toward our Lord Jesus Christ."

John 2:2 says, Jesus Christ "is the propitiation for our sins: and not for ours only, but also for the sins of the whole world." Matthew 18:11 says, "For the Son of man is come to save that which was lost." Finally, you have these classic verses, John 3:16-17, "For God so loved the world, that he gave his only begotten Son, that whosoever believeth in him should not perish, but have everlasting life. For God sent not his Son into the world to condemn the world; but that the world through him might be saved."

We understand through Scripture that the Son of God became the Son of Man so that the sons of man might become the sons of God.

FACT 6 – Salvation is forever.

The question is often raised, can a person once saved become lost again? I am not going to get into Calvinism, which supports eternal security, or Arminianism, which is in opposition to eternal security. I am going to give you biblical facts that support the concept that salvation is forever.

The trinity supports "once saved, always saved." John 10:29 says, "My Father, which gave them me, is greater than all; and no man is able to pluck them out of my Father's hand." 1 Corinthians 1:8-9 says, "Who shall also confirm you unto the end, that ye may be blameless in the day of our Lord Jesus Christ. God is faithful, by whom ye were called unto the fellowship of his Son Jesus Christ our Lord." Verse 8 says "Who shall also confirm you..." This word *confirm* is *bebaios* in Greek, which means *to make firm, to establish, and make secure.*

If you read 1 Corinthians 1:8 using the Greek it would read, "Who shall also secure you unto the end..." God is faithful. Salvation has nothing to do with our faithfulness. Salvation is of the Lord. The work of the Son is spelled out in John 6:37: "All that the Father giveth me shall come to me; and him that cometh to me I will in no wise cast out."

Did you accept the invitation of Jesus and take Him as your Savior? Then He will never cast you out. You belong to Him forever, for all time, and eternity.

The work of the Holy Spirit is clear in Ephesians 4:30: "And grieve not the holy Spirit of God, whereby ye are sealed unto the day of redemption." This is God's seal on every believer, and the Holy Spirit is the glue that holds it fast. It cannot be broken. The Holy Spirit of God is the earnest of our inheritance. In other words, He is the Keeper of our souls.

Revelation 3:5 says, "He that overcometh, the same shall be clothed in white raiment; and I will not blot out his name out of the *Book of Life,* but I will confess his name before my Father, and before his angels." 1 John 5:4-5 says, "For whosoever is born of God overcometh the world: and this is the victory that overcometh the world, even our faith. Who is he that overcometh the world, but he that believeth that Jesus is the Son of God?"

1 John 4:4 says, "Ye are of God, little children, and have overcome them: because greater is He that is in you, than he that is in the world." The possibility of losing one's salvation is not mentioned here. Rather this is an affirmation that those who are born again possess eternal life, and no person or thing can ever separate Christians from the love of God and eternal life.

Jesus says in Revelation 3:5, "I will confess his name before my Father, and before His angels." This promises you eternal citizenship. Christ is your advocate. He is your representative before God, and He will acknowledge your name before the Father. You have a reserved seat in Heaven waiting for you.

So then, can a saved person ever be lost? Absolutely not. If he could, then he would be forced to admit to unthinkable things. The first one is that it is possible for one who has been purged from sin by the blood of Christ to become unpurged. Hebrews 1:3 says, "Who being the brightness of His glory, and the express image of His person, and upholding all things by the word of His power, when He had by himself purged our sins, sat down on the right hand of the Majesty on high."

Another thing you would have to admit is that God does remember that which He promised to forget. Hebrews 10:17 says, "And their sins and iniquities will I remember no more."

You would be forced to believe that it is possible for one who has been sealed to become unsealed. This idea is refuted by Ephesians 4:30: "And grieve not the Holy Spirit of God, whereby ye are sealed unto the day of the redemption."

Another is that God did not really mean you will never be judged. This is refuted by John 5:24: "Verily, verily, I say unto you, He that heareth my word, and believeth on Him that sent me, hath everlasting life, and shall not come into condemnation; but is passed from death unto life."

Another is that God did not really mean you will never taste death. This idea is refuted by John 8:52: "Then said the Jews unto Him, Now we know that thou has a devil. Abraham is dead, and the prophets; and thou sayeth, If a man keep my saying, he shall never taste of death."

Another one is that God did not really mean "shall never be forsaken." This is refuted by Hebrews 13:5: "Let your conversation be without covetousness; and be content with such things as ye have: for He hath said, I will never leave thee, nor forsake thee."

When a person gets saved, their future is always better than their past.

FACT 7 – We have assurance of salvation.

1 John 5:10-13 says, "He that believeth on the Son of God hath the witness in himself: he that believeth not God hath made Him a liar; because he believeth not the record that God gave of His Son." God keeps records, according to verse 11, "And this is the record, that God hath given to us eternal life, and this life is in His Son. He that hath the Son hath life; and he that hath not the Son of God hath not life. These things have I written unto you that believe on the name of the Son of God; that ye may know that ye have eternal life, and that ye may believe on the name of the Son of God."

If you have accepted Jesus Christ into your heart as your own personal Savior, the erros tense of the Greek says "that you may believe on the name of the Son of God and that you may definitely know that you have eternal life."

2 Corinthians 13:5 tells us, "Examine yourselves, whether ye be in the faith; prove your own selves. Know ye not your own selves, how that Jesus Christ is in you, except ye be reprobates." That word *reprobate* means *hopelessly sinful*. We are to examine ourselves. This isn't a guess or a hope or a supposition.

I have four W's when you are examining yourself:
1. When
2. Where
3. Who
4. What

When did you get saved? Where did you get saved? Who was instrumental in leading you to the Lord? What were the circumstances when you got saved? Were you in a church? Were you in an evangelistic service? Were you in somebody's home? What were the circumstances?

In his excellent book on salvation, Dr. Robert Gromacki lists 11 ways by which one may test his salvation experience.
1. Have you enjoyed spiritual fellowship with God, with Christ, and with fellow believers?
2. Do you have a sensitivity to sin?
3. Are you basically obedient to the commandments of Scripture?
4. What is your attitude toward the world and its values?
5. Do you love Jesus Christ and look forward to His coming? Are you looking for that blessed hope?
6. Do you sin less now that you have professed faith in Christ?
7. Do you love other believers?
8. Have you experienced answered prayer?
9. Do you have the inner witness of the Holy Spirit? For instance, the inner witness that you have the assurance of your salvation? Do you have that inner conviction when you are caught up in sin?
10. Do you have the ability to discern between spiritual truth and error?
11. Do you believe the basic doctrines of the faith?

Biblical salvation is the only way to Heaven and eternal life. I certainly hope you have experienced God's marvelous plan of salvation in your life.

CHAPTER 8 | **FACTS 50-56**

7 Vocabulary Words of
Salvation

Many words are used to explain salvation. You read them in the Bible. You hear them from the pulpit. What I've done is choose seven words that I believe are very important words that describe God's marvelous plan of salvation.

1. Reconciliation.

The first word I would like to consider is reconciliation. We hear this word a lot outside of the area of salvation. The Greek word for reconciliation is an easy one to remember, *allasso*. It means *to change from an enemy to a friend*. Colossians 1:21 tells us, "And you, that were sometime alienated (that is separated) and enemies in your mind by wicked works, yet now hath he (that's the Lord Jesus Christ) reconciled." According to 2 Corinthians 5:19, "God was in Christ, reconciling the world unto Himself" at Calvary. God did not change, for He has always loved the sinner.

Nor was the sinner changed, for he continues in sinful rebellion against God. But by the death of Christ on the Cross, the relationship between God and the sinner was changed. The sin barrier that separates a sinner from God was taken away enabling a righteous God, who hates sin, to show mercy upon the sinner where judgment was deserved. The work of this reconciliation was of God alone. Man had no part in it. Christ also brought reconciliation to the sinner whereby he changes his rebellious attitude toward God, and he is now able to be persuaded to accept Christ as his personal Savior.

2. Propitiation.

The second word I want to consider is the word propitiation. Romans 3:25 says, "Whom God hath set forth to be a propitiation (that is the Lord Jesus Christ) through faith in his blood." 1 John 2:2 says, "And He (Jesus) is the propitiation for our sins: and not for ours only, but also for the sins of the whole world." We find in 1 John 4:10, "Herein is love, not that we love God, but that He loved us, and sent his Son to be the propitiation for our sins." A holy and righteous God demanded a holy and righteous sacrifice for your sin and my sin. He could not accept the blood of lambs or bulls and goats. Hebrews 10:4 says, "For it is not possible that the blood of bulls and goats should take away sin. "When Jesus Christ, the sinless Lamb of God, died on Calvary's Cross for your sin and my sin, God was appeased. God was completely satisfied, and Christ met the just demands of a holy and righteous God. His death was sanctioned, approved, and accepted as payment for your sin and my sin.

Propitiation means *to cover up, to remit, to pass over, to show mercy, to satisfy, to appease.* By the sacrifice of Christ, the person who accepts Him as his or her personal Savior, is by God's own act delivered from justly deserved condemnation. He now comes under the grace and mercy of God and is forgiven from sin by the sacrifice of Christ. God is now free to show mercy to the believing sinner, remove his guilt, and remit (or pass over) his sin. The sin barrier, which separated man from God, has been broken down. He has removed it. Christ has become the propitiation, the payment, for our sin, and we are forgiven forever. Not for a time, not as long as you hold on, not as long as you live a good life. It is forever. Romans 8 tells us there is no condemnation, no separation to those who are in Christ Jesus. Hebrews 9:12 says Christ has obtained eternal redemption for us. John 5:11-13 says, "And this is the record, that God hath given us eternal life, and this life is in the Son. He that hath the Son hath life; and he that hath not the Son of God hath not life. These things have I written unto you that believe on the name of the Son of God; that ye may know that ye have eternal life, and that ye may believe on the name of the Son of God." The Lord Jesus Christ has satisfied the demands of a holy and righteous God for our sin through His sacrifice (that's His death on the Cross). He has paid our sin debt by taking our sins from us and bearing it (or carrying it) in Himself upon His own body. By the shedding of His blood, we have been redeemed! We have been purchased! We have been bought back by God from when Adam sold us out to Satan in the garden. Jesus paid it all; all to Him I owe.

In my studies through the years, I have come upon three classic Latin terms that describe propitiation. The first term is *posse pacere*, which is *able to sin*. The second term is *posse non-pacere*, which is *able not to sin*. The third term is *non-posse pacere*, which is *not able to sin*. *Posse pacere* refers to an unsaved person, a person who has never accepted Christ as their Savior. They are able to sin. They continue to sin. There is no conscience about them and what they are doing in their life. This is the natural thing, and they continue in sin. But when a person gets saved, this Latin term *posse non pacere* comes into being, *able not to sin*. We are able to resist sin through the indwelling of the Spirit of God, who is in our heart and in our life since we've become saved. The third term is *non-posse pacere*, which is *not able to sin*. All believers will experience this when they get to Heaven and receive their glorified bodies. They will be just like the Lord Jesus Christ, and they will not be able to sin.

3. Redemption.

The third word I would like to consider is redemption. Here the Greek word is *exagorazo*, which means to *buy out of the marketplace*. We are seen as slaves to sin in the marketplace of this world, and the Lord Jesus Christ comes into the marketplace of this world and pays the price for us. He redeems us. He purchases us. He buys us back unto Himself, and not only does He redeem us, He removes us. He extricates us, He extracts us, and He relocates us out of the marketplace. Then He compassionately *lutroos* us. He releases us from sin. He sets us free from sin. He cuts the cord of sin that entangles us and that has us bound to this world. He emancipates us. We are free. We are set at liberty, which James talks about. We no longer have to have sin rule and reign in our mortal bodies. We are *posse non-pacere*, able not to sin.

4. Imputation.

The fourth word I would like to consider is imputation. What a marvelous word! What great extent has Almighty God gone to, to bring about this wonderful and marvelous plan of salvation! Romans 4:8 says, "Blessed is the man to whom the Lord will not impute sin." *Impute* is a banking term. It means *to place to one's account*. Romans 4:8 could read, "Blessed is the man who does not have his sins placed to his account."

God performs three acts of imputation. The first act is when Adam and Eve sinned in the garden. As they were our representatives, God took their sin and imputed it to the whole human race. Romans 5:12 tells us, "By one man sin entered into the world, and death by sin; and so death passed upon all men, for that all have sinned." The second act of imputation is when the Lord Jesus Christ died on the Cross of Calvary. He took the sins of the whole world and imputed them to Christ. 1 Peter 2:24 says, "Who his own self bare our sins in his own body on the tree." Isaiah 53:5 says, "He was wounded for our transgressions, he was bruised for our iniquities; the chastisement for our peace was upon him; and with his stripes we are healed." The Lord laid on Him (imputed to Him) the iniquity of us all, for He bore our sins upon Himself on the Cross."

When a person finally realizes that he is a sinner, that Christ became his sin bearer on the Cross, and he accepts Jesus as his personal Savior, God does His third act of imputation. He takes the righteousness of the Lord Jesus Christ and imputes it to that person's account. Abraham believed God, and it was imputed to him for righteousness (James 2:23). 2 Corinthians 5:21 says, "For he hath made him to be sin for us, who knew no sin; that we might be made the righteousness of God in him." Romans 3:22 tells us righteousness is for all. God would have all men to be saved. He has no pleasure in the death of the wicked, but His righteousness only comes to rest upon those who believe. God places righteousness to your account only if you have believed and been saved by the Lord Jesus Christ. God seals us with the righteousness of Jesus Christ. We are His forever. Only the righteous will inherit the Kingdom of Heaven. Matthew 25:46 says, "And these shall go away into everlasting punishment: but the righteous into life eternal."

5. Justification.

The fifth word I would like to consider is justification. This word is one of the three words that make up the triangle of salvation. Job asked, "How then can a man be justified with God?" (Job 25:4). As soon as a person receives Christ by faith as his or her Savior, God, by His grace, justifies him. Justification is the legal act whereby man's status before God is changed for the good. A saved person stands justified before God, just as if he'd never sinned. When you get saved, God pronounces you a righteous person and treats you as a righteous person. He adopts you into His family, and you become the Son of God, a child of the King. It is not by works of righteousness that you have done. It's what God does by imputing to you the righteousness of the Lord Jesus Christ, which in turn justifies you before the Throne of God.

6. Sanctification.

The sixth word to consider is sanctification. 1 Thessalonians 5:23 says, "And the very God of peace sanctify you wholly." Sanctification is not the eradication of your sinful nature, which places you in the state of sinless perfection, nor is it the "second blessing," which supposedly places you on a higher godly level than other believers. It is not the baptism of the Holy Spirit, which supposedly gives you the ability to interpret and speak in tongues. Biblical *sanctification*, simply means *to set apart*. The moment you receive Jesus as your Savior, you are sanctified. God sets you apart from this world. You are now a child of God. You are set apart to live a life pleasing unto the Lord. You are set apart for serving the Lord and using the gifts that He has given you. I personally believe in progressive sanctification, which means the more you are involved in the things of the Lord (Bible study, prayer, service unto Him), the more you are set apart from this world's system. You get closer to God's heavenly system, and the Lord uses you more. John the Baptist tells us the more He (Christ) increases, the more we decrease. Salvation is the miracle of a moment, but the growth of a saint is the work of a lifetime. The Spirit of God uses the Word of God to make us more like the Son of God. The closer you get to Jesus, the more the things of this earth will grow strangely dim in the light of His glory and grace.

7. Glorification.

The last word to consider is glorification. Romans 8:30 says, "Moreover whom he did predestinate, them He also called: and whom He called, them He also justified: and whom he justified them, He also glorified." Glorification refers to the ultimate and absolute physical, mental, and spiritual perfection of all believers. It will begin at the Rapture and continue throughout all eternity. Glorification is both the logical and necessary final side of the great salvation triangle. It completes justification and sanctification. Justification saves us from the penalty of sin. Sanctification sets us apart from the power of sin. Glorification will someday remove us from the presence of sin that is non-posse pacere (not able to sin). God has made us to sit together in heavenly places in Christ Jesus (Ephesians 2:6). Romans 8:1 says, "There is therefore now no condemnation to them which are in Christ Jesus." No condemnation. This has been secured by Christ for the believer and has not, and cannot, be broken. Hebrews 2:3 says, "How shall we escape, if we neglect so great salvation?" Salvation is of the Lord and is a marvelous plan designed by God Himself. We had no part in it. Christ died in our place to save ordinary people for an extraordinary destiny in the world to come.

CHAPTER 9 | FACTS 57-63

7 Blessings of
Salvation

Hebrews 2:3 states, "How shall we escape, if we neglect so great salvation?" What a marvelous and wonderful salvation God has given us by grace through faith in the Lord Jesus Christ! These seven blessings are found in Revelation 2 and 3 and are given to everyone who is saved. These chapters include the seven letters that were written to the seven churches in Paul's day. These churches were actual Bible-believing churches.

BLESSING 1 – Eternal life.

The first blessing is found in Revelation 2:7, which is part of the letter to the first church, the church at Ephesus. The passage says, "He that hath an ear, let him hear what the Spirit saith unto the churches; To him that overcometh will I give to eat of the tree of life, which is in the midst of the paradise of God." (The first phrase in every blessing is "He that overcometh.") The word *overcometh* does not refer to Christians who have gained some spiritual victories in life from some trials and tribulations. It is referring to those who have accepted Christ as their own personal Savior.

Revelation 12:11 tells us, "And they overcame him by the blood of the Lamb, and by the word of their testimony; and they loved not their lives unto the end." 1 John 5:4-5 states, "For whatsoever is born of God overcometh the world: and this is the victory that overcometh the world, even our faith. Who is he that overcometh the world, but he that believeth that Jesus is the Son of God?" 1 John 4:4 states, "Ye are of God, little children, and have overcome them: because greater is he that is in you, than he that is in the world."

This is talking about saved people. True believers are assured of eternal life. They will eat of the Tree of Life that was first mentioned in the Garden of Eden and is now in Heaven. Those who eat of the Tree will live forever. Genesis 3:22 says, "And the Lord God said, Behold, the man is become as one of us, to know good and evil: and now, lest he put forth his hand, and take also of the tree of life, and eat, and live forever."

BLESSING 2 – Resurrection.

The second blessing is found in the same chapter, Revelation 2, this time in verse 11. It is the letter to the second church, the church at Smyrna. This blessing says, "He that hath an ear, let him hear what the Spirit saith unto the churches; He that overcometh shall not be hurt of the second death." In Revelation 20:6 we read about this second death, "Blessed and holy is he that hath part in the first resurrection: on such the second death has no power, but they shall be priests of God and of Christ, and shall reign with him one thousand years."

This is the resurrection of all saved — Old Testament, New Testament, and Tribulation saints — to Heaven. There are two deaths and two resurrections. The first resurrection is for the righteous. The second resurrection is for the wicked. These resurrections will happen 1,000 years apart. Believers who die before the Rapture are taken to Heaven when their time is up on this earth. They suffer a physical death; that is the first death. These believers are in the first resurrection. Unbelievers are in the second resurrection and will experience the second death. They will experience the first death, which is a physical death, and they will experience the second death, which is a spiritual death. These are the people who reject Jesus Christ as their Savior. They are cast away from God, away from His presence, cast into outer darkness forever and ever. No true believer will have to stand before the Great White Throne Judgment and be condemned to the Lake of Fire, which is the second death (Revelation 20:15).

BLESSING 3 – Spiritual sustenance, acceptance, and a new name.

The third blessing is found in Revelation 2:17, a passage that was written to the church at Pergamos. "He that hath an ear, let him hear what the Spirit saith unto the churches; To him that overcometh will I give to eat of the hidden manna, and will give him a white stone, and in the stone a new name written, which no man knoweth saving he that receiveth it."

Here the believer is promised three things:

1. They will eat hidden manna. Christ, who is the bread of life and the living word, provides spiritual sustenance for believers. By the Holy Spirit living within us, we are able to discern and understand the Word of God and can grow to spiritual maturity. We have a live-in Bible teacher through the Holy Spirit.
2. They will be given a white stone. This is a symbol of Christ's assurance and acceptance to all who have not succumbed to Satan's deception and rebellion. "Wherefore we labour, that,

whether present or absent, we may be accepted of Him" 2 Corinthians 5:9. "And hath raised us up together, and made us sit together in heavenly places in Christ Jesus" (Ephesians 2:6).
3. They will be given a new name. This is a symbol of the personal and intimate relationship believers will experience with the Lord in Heaven. We give our children names. In like manner the Lord will give each one of us a new name. This name is assurance to the believer that he is a child of God and that he belongs to the family of God. Ephesians 1:13 says, "In whom ye also trusted, after that ye heard the Word of Truth, the Gospel of your salvation: in whom also after that ye believed, ye were sealed with the Holy Spirit of promise." You became a child of God. There is a new name written down in Glory, and it's mine, oh yes, it's mine!

BLESSING 4 – The privilege to reign with Christ and the "morning star."

The fourth blessing is found in Revelation 2:26-28. Two promises are given here to the believer. They will be given power over the nations. Saved people will be given authority to rule over the nations during the Millennium, the 1,000 years (Revelation 20:6), sharing the privilege granted to Christ by God the Father. The redeemed of the Lord will return, rule, and reign with Him. The people we will be ruling over will be the "sheep nations." These "sheep nations" are found in Matthew 25. These are the people who have lived through the Tribulation. They are people who have been saved in the Tribulation by the preaching of the 144,000 (Revelation 7), and these are people who were friends of the Jews when they were being persecuted by the Antichrist during the Tribulation. Believers will not only execute judgment but will administer mercy, direction, and protection to the nations during the Kingdom Age. I must say this: No unsaved person will enter into the 1,000 years.

The second promise is they will be given the morning star. Jesus has given Himself to the believer, and at the Rapture He will appear over this dark world to take believers away before the Tribulation. Jesus will reappear to usher in the dawn of the new Millennium (1,000 years) at His second coming, and we will be part of that morning star revelation.

BLESSING 5 – Righteousness and your name written in the *Book of Life*.

The fifth blessing is found in Revelation 3:5. This is in the letter to the church at Sardis. "He that overcometh (gets saved), the same shall be clothed in white raiment; and I will not blot out his name out of the *Book of Life*, but I will confess his name before my Father, and before His angels."

Three promises are given in this passage:
1. White raiment. It is a symbol of purity and righteousness. It is the garment of salvation. It is the garment of the saved. The moment you got saved, righteousness was imputed to you. It was placed to your account. This is the righteousness of the Lord Jesus Christ. God justified you. He pronounced you a righteous person, and he treats you as a righteous person, not a sinner. When you accepted Christ as your personal Savior, you were immediately clothed in white raiment. The blood of the Lord Jesus Christ has made you whiter than snow.
2. He will not blot your name out of the *Book of Life*. The *Book of Life* is mentioned many times in the Scriptures. In Exodus 32:32, Moses was up on the mountain receiving the Ten Commandments from God. As he was descending from the mountain, he found the children of Israel worshipping a golden calf. Moses stated, that if God would not forgive them, he wanted his name blotted out of the *Book of Life*.

God keeps books. I told you in the last chapter about the record book God keeps (1 John 5). David talked about God's books in Psalm 139. It seems God has a book for each person who is conceived. All these together make up the *Book of Life* — one great volume containing the names and deeds of everyone who was ever given biological life. Everyone will be judged according to the things written in God's book. Saved people will be judged at the Judgment Seat of Christ (Romans 14:10, 2 Corinthians 5:10). This is a judgment for rewards. Unsaved people will be judged at the Great White Throne judgment of Revelation 20:11-12. The things written in God's book will decide and prove their eternal destiny by a just God. In Psalm 69:28, David talks about the adversaries of God, "Let them be blotted out of the book of the living (Book of Life), and not be written with the righteous." In Daniel 12:1, the Jews to be delivered will be those found written in the *Book of Life*. This deliverance will occur at the end of the book of Revelation or at the end of the Tribulation as they (Jewish people) will receive Jesus Christ as their Messiah. Philippians 4:3 says to help fellow Christians whose names are in the *Book of Life*.

Revelation 13:8 says that all who dwell upon the earth whose names are not written in the *Book of Life* will worship the Antichrist. Revelation 17:18 notes that people during the Tribulation whose names are not in the *Book of Life* will wonder about the Antichrist. Revelation 20:15 says, "And whosoever was not found written in the *Book of Life* was cast into the lake of fire."

Further on Revelation 21:27 says no one shall enter into heaven; only those whose names are in the *Lamb's Book of Life*. Those whose names will not be blotted out of the

Book of Life will only be those who are saved, who have been redeemed with the precious blood of Christ without blemish and without spot. *God's Book of Life* will become the *Lamb's Book of Life* in which is written forever all those saved and redeemed by His blood.

Here is my question to you: Is your name written in the *Lamb's Book of Life*? John 3:15 says, "That whosoever believeth in him should not perish, but have eternal life." The one who is trusting Jesus Christ as Savior and Lord has many wonderful possessions, which cannot be seen with our physical eyes, but which are as real and permanent as if we were already in Heaven. Many of these are known by the present tense of the verb *have*; not *might have*, not *could have*. We who believe in Him *have* (right now) eternal life. Our sins have been taken care of by the sacrificial death of Christ in whom we have redemption through His blood. Ephesians 2:5-6 says, "Even when we were dead in sins, hath quickened us together with Christ, (by grace ye are saved;) And hath raised us up together, and made us sit together in heavenly places in Christ Jesus." In these two marvelous verses, the word *together* appears three times referring in each case to our spiritual union with Jesus Christ. The word is in combination with other words. The first combination is *quickened us together,* which means *made alive with*. The second combination is *raised us up together,* which means we *are resurrected with*. The third combination is *made us sit together,* which means we are *already seated with*. All of these verbs are given in the past tense stressing that as far as God's own word is concerned, we have been already seated eternally in the heavens with Christ. Our Lord will confess you before his heavenly Father and before His angels.

BLESSING 6 – The believer will escape the Tribulation, have security, and have God's signature on him.

The sixth blessing is found in Revelation 3:12 in the letter written to the church at Philadelphia. "Him that overcometh will I make a pillar in the temple of my God, and he shall go no more out: and I will write upon him the name of my God, and the name of the city of my God, which is new Jerusalem, which cometh down out of Heaven from my God: and I will write upon him my new name."

This blessing involves three promises:

1. In Revelation 3:10 the believer and the church are promised by our Lord that we will not go through the seven-year Tribulation. He will keep us from the hour of temptation (Tribulation), which will come upon all the world. Note: I have been tempted by Satan many times in this life, and so have you. This word temptation here is really rendered *Tribulation*.

2. The believer is promised security in Him. The believer "will I make a pillar in the temple of my God, and he shall go no more out." As an architect I can tell you that a pillar is used for structural stability in a building. You cannot remove it. A pillar in the Temple of God symbolizes salvation, spiritual stability, and eternal security of never being separated from the shelter of God's presence. In other words, you are secure in Christ. There is no condemnation, no separation from the love of Christ. He will never leave you nor forsake you. You belong to Him forever because He bought you with a great price.

3. The signature of God will be inscribed upon every believer. "I will write upon him the name of my God, and the name of the city of my God … and My new name." This statement brings to my mind a ranch owner branding the cattle

that belong to him. These names inscribed upon the saved person signify total identification with and ownership by God. It ensures the believer of an eternal place in His kingdom. We have been branded by the Lord and are His forever. In sharp contrast to the Lake of Fire, the future home of all of the unsaved, the Bible also promises a wonderful city as the future home of all saved people, the Bride of Christ. It is called the Holy City, and the description of the city is found in the last two chapters of Revelation. Revelation 21:11-16 tells us it is a city shining. It has 12 pearly gates, it has 12 foundations, it is foursquare and 12,000 furlongs. Computing these measurements, this city will be approximately 1,400 miles wide, 1,400 miles deep, and 1,400 miles high. (One furlong equals 582 feet.) It will be of pure gold, like crystal glass. The streets will be pure gold and will be transparent. Mansions will be there. It is fascinating to note that the Bible predicts more than just one future age. Ephesians 2:7 says, "That in the ages to come he might shew the exceeding riches of his grace in his kindness toward us through Christ Jesus." We do not know about these ages yet, but what a wonderful time of fellowship as well as service awaits us in that beautiful city! One of the greatest and most wonderful aspects of the ages to come in God's Holy City is there will be no defilements. Whatever you do, don't miss it!

BLESSING 7 – We will reign with Christ for 1,000 years on this earth.

The seventh blessing is found in Revelation 3:21. Jesus Christ is writing to the church at Laodicea, the last church to which Jesus Christ wrote these letters. These seven churches have also been seen as representative of church periods down through the ages of time since Jesus Christ was crucified on the Cross.

We are in the Age of Grace, but we are also in the Church Age. God is working through the Church Age. The church is home base. Everything that God does today on this earth is through the church. We are in the Laodicean Church Age, which is the last Church Age.

Revelation 3:21 tells us, "To him that overcometh will I grant to sit with me in my throne, even as I also overcame, and am set down with my Father in his throne." Christ promises to those who are born again that He will grant them to sit with Him on His throne. Saved believers will share the throne of their Savior, the Lord Jesus Christ. Jesus is now seated at the right hand of God the Father. A joint reign with Christ is mentioned a number of times throughout Revelation. All believers are joint heirs with Christ. During the Millennium, Christ will establish His throne on the earth, and all believers will reign with Him for 1,000 years. We will also be with Him and serve Him throughout all eternity. Can there be any greater reward than this? I can only give God all the thanks and praise for so great a salvation!

CHAPTER 10 | **FACTS 64-70**

7 Walks of
The Believer

The Bible says that as Christians we walk in this world as strangers because our citizenship is in Heaven not in this world. *Walk* is a very common Hebrew word. The word *walk* denotes *conduct of daily living*. The word *walk* is a descriptive word. It describes who we are, what we do, how we act, how we think, and where we go. It's a life described by one word — **walk.** People know you by your walk. 1 John 2:6 says, "He that saith he abideth in him ought himself also so to walk, even as He walked."

The idea of walking as Christ walked can be intimidating to a Christian. For Christ has set an exceedingly high standard. Nothing short of perfection and total sacrifice will do. Nevertheless, while we recognize that we will never fully achieve sinless perfection on this side of Heaven, the Bible tells us in Colossians 2:6, "As ye have therefore received Christ Jesus the Lord, so walk ye in Him."

The Bible gives seven standards of walk for all believers.

STANDARD 1 - Walk in the Spirit.

The first standard is found in Galatians 5:16 and 25. It is walk in the Spirit. We need to be careful here. A lot of Christians misunderstand this and seek something more than what it means. They seek what is known as the second blessing. They want to become hyper spiritual. In other words, they want to be above the normal Christian. There is nothing wrong with wanting to be the very best we can be for Christ by the grace of God, but we cannot think of ourselves as more spiritual than others. We need to be careful we do not get the Holy Spirit above the Lord Jesus Christ. John 15:26 tells us the Holy Spirit will not speak of Himself; He will glorify the Lord Jesus Christ. The Holy Spirit is a comforter. He is an influence. He is the power source of all spiritual energy. The Bible says he is a person. He is intelligent. He knows the deep things of God and reveals them to us. He makes decisions. He gives us gifts distributing to each individual as He will. He is emotional. We are not to grieve the Holy Spirit. He is active. He does things only people can do. He speaks. He intercedes. He teaches, leads, appoints, and empowers. We are not to quench the Spirit of God in our lives. He is God. He is equal with God. He is the third person of the triune nature of God.

Who can have the power to be filled and walk in the Spirit?
1. You must be a born again Christian. In other words, you must be a person who has received Jesus Christ into your heart as your own personal Savior.
2. Only those Christians who want and choose it. Ephesians 5:18 says, "And be not drunk with wine, wherein is excess; but be filled with the Spirit."

So what is the filling of the Holy Spirit? The filling or power of the Holy Spirit is the influence or control the Spirit exercises over us when we yield ourselves to Him. Romans 6:13 tells us we are to yield ourselves to God. The Holy Spirit does not overpower us. We receive all of the Spirit of God we are going to get when we are saved. The Holy Spirit regenerates, indwells, baptizes, and seals us. (This is what we call R.I.B.S.) Only when we submit to Him does He begin to control us. I pray almost every day for the filling of the Holy Spirit and his influence in my life, so I will be controlled by Him. When God gave the Holy Spirit to the church on the day of Pentecost, believers spoke in all of the known languages in Jerusalem. The people who were around the apostles and heard them speaking in these different languages said they were drunk with wine. A person who is drunk with wine will walk, talk, act, think, and feel in a different manner. Alcohol's control results in impaired judgment. On the other hand a person who is filled with the Holy Spirit will walk, talk, act, think, and feel in a different manner. The Spirit's control results in improved judgment.

How can you be filled with and walk in the Spirit? This involves four essentials on your part:
1. You must be Christ-centered.
2. You must be in the Word.
3. You must be submissive.
4. You must be confident.

We must focus our attention on the Lord Jesus Christ. We must spend time in the Word of God. We must have an attitude of submissiveness. When you have done these three, you must trust God that He is faithful to do His part; therefore, giving you confidence that you are walking in the Spirit.

How can you tell when you are walking in the Spirit? There are four ways:
1. You have joyful fellowship.
2. You have heartfelt praise. Your heart magnifies the Lord.
3. You have an abounding gratitude for the grace of God that has saved you.
4. You are reverent in submission. It is not your will but His will. He must increase, and you must decrease.

Galatians 5:22 points out that the life of a Christian who is walking in the Spirit will be marked by nine moral qualities known as the fruit of the Spirit.
1. Love. That is putting God and others ahead of ourselves.
2. Joy. That is a spirit of gladness in our salvation.
3. Peace. That is inner serenity based on what Christ has done for you.
4. Long-suffering. That is patience in the midst of difficult circumstances.
5. Meekness (kindness). That is treating others as we want to be treated.
6. Goodness. That is to be honest, pure, and generous.
7. Faithfulness. That is to be trusted and dependable.
8. Gentleness. That is to be tender, sensitive, and gracious.
9. Temperance (self-control). That is to control our desires.

STANDARD 2 – Walk worthy of God.

The second standard of walking is found in 1 Thessalonians 2:12, "Walk worthy of God." "Walk worthy" is what Paul also wrote to the Ephesians. He said, "I therefore, the prisoner of the Lord, beseech you that ye walk worthy of the vocation wherewith ye are called" (Ephesians 4:1). He continues in Ephesians 4 to outline the walk and service of a believer. The Christian's walk and service are not according to man-made rules or standards. It does not mean that we are supposed to sign a pledge that we will not go here or there nor do this or that. We are to walk worthy of the name Christian. In us Jesus must find his earthly walk. He lives in our hearts. He walks in our bodies, and we are the Bible the world reads. We present the only Christ the world will ever know. If the world does not see Jesus in us, then we are not walking worthy of the Christ that lives within us.

Many people measure Christ by the way we walk. We prove to others by the way we walk that we have had a change of heart and that we are a new creature. We are a new creation in Christ, but more than that, we possess a divine nature. We are to produce righteous living in a righteous walk. The fruit we bear outwardly testifies to what we possess inwardly. As spiritually minded believers, we are to be imitators of Christ. We are read by people whether we know it or not. They watch us, listen to us when we talk, and check the places we go, the things we do, and the company we keep. As representatives of the Lord Jesus Christ in a wicked world, we should be very careful how we walk. The old saying goes, "You can't talk the talk if you don't walk the walk."

STANDARD 3 – Walk by faith.

The third standard of walk for the Christian is found in 2 Corinthians 5:7: "We are supposed to walk by faith." Our God is invisible, but we know God is there. We cannot see God the Father. We cannot see the Lord Jesus Christ seated at the right hand of God. And we cannot see the person of the Holy Spirit. No one on earth today has literally seen Heaven, but true believers know that God is, Christ is, the Holy Spirit is, and Heaven is a real place. We know it because God said so, and we believe God. We walk by faith not by sight. What we see we do not need faith to believe or accept. Things eternal are not seen. We are saved by God's grace through faith, so faith brings saving grace. Faith imputes, or places to our account, the righteousness of the Lord Jesus Christ, and righteousness only comes to rest upon those who have faith, or in other words, believe. We are justified by faith. We walk by faith. And whatsoever is not of faith is sin, so therefore the Christian life is a life of faith. We trust and believe God simply because God is God, and He cannot do any wrong. He cannot break the promise. By like token believers are not governed by things that can be seen. Our daily pattern of life is influenced and controlled by those things which we do not see. Faith determines the way we live. Faith is "Forsaking **All** **I** **T**rust **H**im."

STANDARD 4 – Walk in love.

Our fourth standard of walk is found in Ephesians 5:2. We are to walk in love. If you walk in love, you please God. God is love. So it is logical that a child of God will walk in love. In fact the Father loves us as He loves His Son (John 17:23). We are born into a loving relationship with the Father that ought to result in our showing love to Him by the way we live and walk. Ephesians 3:17 says our spiritual lives are rooted and grounded in love. He has purchased us with a great price. John 15:13 says, "Greater love hath no man than this, that a man lay down his life for his friends." Our love for Him is our response to His love for us. The plan of love to which we are lifted is the love that Christ exhibited when He loved us enough to give Himself as an offering and sacrifice for us on the Cross.

If God treated mankind like some Christians treat each other and like some Christians treat their families, friends, and neighbors, this earth would be a place of untold agony. We must forbear one another in love no matter what the circumstances and provocations are. Ephesians 4:2 says, "With all lowliness and meekness, with long-suffering, forbearing one another in love."

Jesus loved His enemies. He did not compromise with them. He did not love their sin, but He loved them. The essence of Christianity is love. If we do not love our fellow man whom we see, how can we love God whom we cannot see? (I John 4:20). Remember that love is the first on the list of fruit of the Spirit. So we are to walk in love because love is the fundamental factor in the Christian life. If we walk in love, we will not disobey God or injure men because He that loves another has fulfilled the law, and the Holy Spirit puts this love in our hearts. "Because the love of God is shed abroad in our hearts by the Holy Ghost which is given unto us (Romans 5:5)." He has chosen us in love, and rooted, and grounded us in love. Now we should forbear one another and build one another up in love, speak the truth in love, and walk daily in His love.

STANDARD 5 – Walk in the light.
The fifth walk is found in Ephesians 5:8. We are to walk in the light. Since God is light and we are imitating our Heavenly Father, then we should walk in the light and have nothing to do with the darkness of sin. We are sanctified, or set apart ones, and no longer belong to the world of darkness (sin) around us. We have been *lutrooed*; which means *we have been set free from the sin that used to bind us, and we have been "called out of darkness into his marvelous light"* 1 Peter 2:9. The light produces goodness, which is a fruit of the Spirit. Jesus said, "Let your light so shine before men, that they may see your good works, and glorify your Father, which is in Heaven (Matthew 5:16). Everyone that doeth evil hateth the light, neither cometh to the light, lest his deeds should be reproved. But he that doeth truth cometh to the light, that his deeds may be made manifest, that they are wrought in God" (John 3:20-21).

To walk as children of light means to live before the eyes of God not hiding anything. It is easy to hide things from other people because they cannot see our hearts and minds, but all things are open and naked unto the Lord. He is omniscient. His eyes are upon the righteous, and His ears are open to their prayers (Psalm 34:15). Walking in the light also means revealing God's light in our daily lives. By our character and conduct, we bring God's light into a dark world. As God's lights we help others find their way to Christ. Only as we witness and share Christ with others can the light enter in. As a child of God walking in the light, you can lead a lost person out of darkness into God's wonderful light. Light reveals God. Light produces fruit. As we walk in the light, we refuse to fellowship with darkness. When you think of light, you think of waking up to a new day. Salvation is the beginning of a new day, and we ought to live as those who belong to light not to the darkness. The believer has no business in the darkness because he "hath delivered us from the power of darkness, and hath translated us into the kingdom of his dear Son" (Colossians 1:13). So having said all of this, therefore, we should walk in the light.

STANDARD 6 – Walk circumspectly.

Our sixth standard of walk is found in Ephesians 5:15-16. We should walk circumspectly. Circumspect comes from two Latin words that mean *looking around*. The Greek word carries the idea of precision and accuracy. See that you walk *carefully with exactness* is the meaning, taking advantage of the God-given circumstances. The opposite would be walking carelessly and without proper guidance. We cannot leave the Christian life to chance. We must make wise decisions and seek to do the will of God. In verse 14 Paul appears to be saying, "Don't walk in your sleep. Wake up. Open your eyes. Make the most of the day." Many Christians go through life sleepwalking. We are not to walk as fools. Only a fool drifts with the wind and the tide. We are not to be driven about with every wind of doctrine (Ephesians 4:14). We all need to look carefully at how we walk. We are to walk wisely because we have the spirit and wisdom of God. We need to plan our work and then work the plan. We are not to waste time. We need to use every opportunity the Lord gives us wisely. *Opportunity* means *toward the port*. It suggests a ship taking advantage of the wind and tide to arrive safely in the harbor. The Apostle Paul says in verse 16 "the days are evil."

The days we live in are much more evil than in Paul's time. We need to walk circumspectly to reveal the urgency of the hour. A Christian ought to walk in such a way that everyone knows they are a child of God without asking them.

STANDARD 7 – Walk in truth.

The seventh standard of walk is found in 3 John 1:4. Walk in truth. The Bible tells us that His truth should be our shield and that His truth endures forever. David said, "I have chosen the way of truth" (Psalm 119:30). As Christians we know that Jesus is the way and the truth (John 14:6), that God would have all men come to the knowledge of the truth (1 Timothy 2:4), and that the truth will set men free (John 8:32). As we live in this world of deception because of Satan, many people are searching and looking for the truth. As we walk in this day, we need to be steadfast and confident that we have the truth, studying and rightly dividing the Word of Truth. We should always be willing and ready to testify for our Lord and give an account of the hope that is within us, speaking the truth in love. Truth brings hope, and hope is what this world needs.

As we grow in the Lord and allow the Holy Spirit to develop these seven walks in us, we will then begin to truly walk with God. Enoch is one of two men (the other is Elijah), who lived on earth and went to Heaven without passing through the veil of death. He is one who lived before the flood, and we know some things about him. His record is found in Genesis 5:21-24. Verse 24 says, "Enoch walked with God." This is a tremendous statement. I would like people to say that about me, and I am sure you would too. Amos 3:3 says, "Can two walk together, except they be agreed?" Enoch was in agreement with God. When a believer walks with God, they are reconciled to God. God is not conformed to him or her, but they are conformed to God.

Their mind is renewed and transformed to the perfect will of God. Walking with God means moral fitness. It means you have fellowship with God. We cease walking our way. We abandon the world's way, and we walk the divine way. Walking with God means to be surrendered to Him. Enoch had a readiness and willingness to do the will of God. He was God's prophet before the flood (Jude 14-15). To walk with God implies spiritual communion with Him. It implies you grow in grace, and your growth is in the knowledge of the Lord. Walking with God gives you a deep, settled joy and peace. It ensures God's protection as He holds you in the hollow of His hand, and you safely abide under His wings. Walking with God implies to be a witness for Him. Jude 14 declares the witness of Enoch.

Hebrews 11:5 tells us Enoch pleased God. Enoch walked with God for 300 years, and God was satisfied with his walk. In fact God was that satisfied with Enoch that He translated him; he took him up to Heaven. The people who knew him (neighbors and friends) searched for him but could not find him. Enoch did not go through the veil of death. Enoch is a type of the believing church, the blood-bought believers who will be here on earth before the Tribulation period. Just as Enoch was taken up to Heaven before the flood without dying, so will the believing church be translated up into Heaven before the Tribulation. The Apostle Paul states in 1 Corinthians 15:51, "Behold, I show you a mystery; We shall not all sleep (die), but we shall be changed." He further states in 1 Thessalonians 4:17, "Then we which are alive and remain shall be caught up together with them in the clouds, to meet the Lord in the air: and so shall we ever be with the Lord."

May it be our desire to walk with God as Enoch did during this short time we have on earth, and may we be among the number that is raptured up into Glory.

CHAPTER 11 | FACTS 71-77

7 Facts About
Prayer

I have a feeling that when we get to Heaven we will find the greatest ministry we had here on earth was prayer. Ian Bounds, who has written much about prayer, says that prayer honors God. It acknowledges His being. It exalts His power. It endues His providence, and it secures His aid. I don't know about your prayer life, but I sense a great need for prayer in people's lives. A few words offered up without much thought is what many people regard as their prayer life. Only in times of desperation or great tragedy is any thought put into the words spoken to the God of the universe.

I would like to give you seven facts about prayer.

FACT 1 – Prayer is invited.

God invites us to pray. The invitation is found throughout the Bible. "Then shall ye call upon me, and ye shall go and pray unto me, and I will hearken unto you" (Jeremiah 29:12). In fact

God enjoins us to pray. He says, "Call unto me," and He encourages us with, "and I will answer thee" (Jeremiah 33:3).

In Luke 18:1, Jesus said men are always to pray and not to faint. That is not to cease, not to stop, and not to slow down. In Philippians 4:6 we are told, "Be careful for nothing; but in every thing by prayer and supplication (humbleness) with thanksgiving let your requests be known to God." You can pray about anything and everything. Peter tells us in 1 Peter 5:7, "Casting all your cares upon Him (Jesus); for He careth for you." God is concerned about every area of our lives. He only wants the best for us.

We are to pray without ceasing. Paul told the Romans in Romans 1:9, "For God is my witness ... that without ceasing I make mention of you always in my prayers." In 1 Thessalonians 1:2-3 Paul says, "We give thanks to God always for you all, making mention of you in our prayers; remembering without ceasing your work of faith, and labour of love, and patience of hope in our Lord Jesus Christ, in the sight of God and our Father." Also in 2 Timothy 1:3, Paul says, "I thank God, whom I serve from my forefathers with a pure conscience, that without ceasing I have remembrance of thee in my prayers night and day."

James tells us in James 5:13, "Is any among you afflicted? let him pray." Are you suffering with some affliction in your life? God invites you to pray about it. Prayer is as old as man. Prayer is universal. Every religion has some sort of prayer. Prayer is a must. Prayer is a privilege. Prayer is talking with God. Prayer is asking and receiving. Prayer is making your requests known to God. Psalm 34:15 says, "The eyes of the Lord are upon the righteous, and his ears are open unto their prayers."

FACT 2 – Prayer is essential.

I tell you the truth: Nothing gets done without prayer. Nothing moves the hand of God like prayer. There is power in prayer.

Prayer will bring the peace of God in your life. Worry destroys peace. Prayer builds confidence. Prayer brings the peace of God, which passes all understanding and keeps your heart and mind through Christ Jesus (Philippians 4:7). You may have gone through a crisis and wondered how you ever got through it. You got through it because people prayed for you. Many times we are put in circumstances where the bottom drops out, and there seems to be no solution. Remember this: The shortest distance between the problem you are facing and the solution is the distance between your knees and the floor. You can always find the solution for your circumstances through prayer.

Prayer should be your first response when you are facing a problem. Many times we try other ways to get the solutions, and they just don't seem to work. I have learned to solve my problems vertically instead of horizontally. You know, whenever I call up there, I never get a busy signal because He invites me to call upon Him.

Jesus cares for you. He is concerned about you. He wants to be part of your life. He wants to be involved in every area of it. Prayer is sharing everything in your life with God. Praying is giving God charge of your life. Praying is depending totally on God. If your prayer life is meager, it is because you consider prayer supplemental and not a necessary fundamental. We have not because we ask not (James 4:2). If you lack in prayer, you lack in power. You are like a sail without wind, a well without water, a car without a steering wheel, a computer without a program. Prayer is essential to a healthy, balanced Christian life.

FACT 3 – Prayer is specific.

Ephesians 5:20 says, "Giving thanks always for all things unto God and the Father in the name of our Lord Jesus Christ." We are to pray in Jesus' name. John 14:13-14 says, "And whatsoever ye shall ask in my name, that will I do, that the Father may be glorified in the Son. If ye shall ask any thing in my name, I will do it." Matthew 6 tells us we are to pray to our Father in Heaven. God is not of this world. He is not limited nor is He bound to the things of this world. He is in Heaven where He has unlimited power, for there is nothing impossible for Him to do. He is all-wise, loving, knowing, and powerful.

Matthew 6 gives us a model prayer or a prototype for praying. We are to pray for His kingdom to come. The New Testament has more than 320 references to the Lord's coming again. His coming again will be in two stages. The first time will be for the church before the Tribulation. From the Cross until this time all of those who have confessed Christ as their Savior will be raptured off this earth. They will be taken off this earth when Jesus comes for His church.

The second time will be after the Tribulation. He will set His kingdom up on earth, and He will rule and reign for 1,000 years (Revelation 20:6). It will be a time when "The earth shall be filled with the knowledge of the glory of the Lord, as the waters cover the seas" (Habakkuk 2:14). And we (the redeemed) will rule and reign with Him (Christ) during the kingdom period. At this time His will will be done on this earth. We are to specifically pray for His coming again. Titus 2:11-15 says we are to pray for that blessed hope and glorious appearing of our great God and Savior, Jesus the King.

Matthew 6:11 tells us we are to pray for our daily necessities. We are to confess and pray for forgiveness of our sins. Unconfessed sin is a hindrance to prayer. We are to judge ourselves. If we say we have no sin, we make Him a liar (1 John 1:10). We will not reach that plane of sinless perfection until we go to Heaven to be with Jesus. We are to pray for the leading of the Lord in our lives and the deliverance and protection from temptation and evil. The devil wants you to fail. The devil wants you to rebel against God. We need to be specific when we pray.

If you pray for missionaries, you need to pray for open doors, for their needs, for their protection, for their families, for their support. We need to pray for widows and widowers. We need to pray for the peace of Jerusalem. Never before in the history of the world do Jerusalem and the country of Israel need our prayers as they do now. We need to pray for our families. We need to pray for young people, for our spouse, for harmony in our marriages. The devil tries to cause disharmony. Unharmonious relationships between husbands and wives hinder prayer (Colossians 3:18-19). We need to pray for one another. James 5:16 tells us, "Confess your faults one to another, and pray for one another, that ye may be healed. The effectual fervent prayer of a righteous man availeth much."

We need to pray for lost people, those around us who have never known Christ. They could be family members, friends, neighbors, or coworkers. Luke 10:2 tells us, "The harvest truly is great, but the labourers are few: pray ye therefore the Lord of the harvest, that He would send forth labourers into His harvest." We need to pray for people to go into the ministry. We need to pray for people who have the gift of soul winning to win souls. We need to pray for missionaries who proclaim the gospel. We are to pray for kings and for all who are in authority over us (our president, the governor, our representatives, your church boards, your church leaders). We need to pray for the ministry of those who proclaim the Gospel. In short, we should offer up supplication, prayers, intercessions, and thanksgiving for all men everywhere. "In every thing give thanks: for this is the will of God in Christ Jesus concerning you" (1 Thessalonians 5:18).

FACT 4 – Prayer is persistent.

Romans 12:12 says, "Rejoicing in hope; patient in tribulation; continuing instant in prayer." "Patient in tribulation, rejoicing in hope," surely portrays a life in close communion with God. The privilege in continuing instant in prayer is possible because of the indwelling of the Holy Spirit in your life. No matter where we are or how softly the prayer is spoken, He is able to hear us. The words *continuing instant* represent one Greek word meaning literally *ever enduring in*. The picture here is one of being always ready to pray whenever the need arises. We need to develop a burden for prayer. We need to realize the importance of prayer concerning everything in our lives.

We need to build an intimate relationship with God through prayer. We need to persevere in prayer. We need to be steadfast in prayer. Prayer is not rushing into God and requesting or petitioning Him for a lot of things and then rushing out. Prayer is being consistent and persistent with God. You may have to wait for an answer, but be persistent to continue to pray for that request. While you wait, don't give up. God will answer you. Hebrews 4:15 tells us, "For we have not an high priest which cannot be touched with the feeling of our infirmities." We need to continue, be persistent, and don't give up on prayer.

The Apostle Paul admonishes us to "pray without ceasing" in 1 Thessalonians 5:17. This does not imply a continual, verbalized prayer but a continual attitude of prayer and watchfulness whereby it becomes easy and natural to breathe a short prayer whenever a need appears. We need to pray for strength in our lives, for guidance, for safety, for protection. So thus whether at work or at rest, we can continue in prayer. We need to be persistent in praying. Whatever you do, don't give up.

FACT 5 – Prayer is vital.

If we want God to move in our lives, in our family's lives, in our church, in our nation, in the world, then prayer is vital. It must be because prayer is the only thing that moves the hand of God. Jesus said we are to pray and not to faint (Luke 18:1). In other words, don't stop. Prayer is the only way to get something from God. James 4:2 tells us, "Ye have not, because ye ask not."

There is joy in prayer. John said in John 16:24, "And ye shall receive, that your joy may be full." Prayer will deliver you out of your troubles. Psalms 34:6 says, "This poor man cried, and the Lord heard him, and saved him out of all his troubles." Prayer can unlock the treasure chest of God's wisdom for you. James 1:5 says, "If any of you lack wisdom, let him ask of God, that giveth to all men liberally." This is a wonderful thing that God gives us through prayer. Prayer is a channel of power. Jeremiah 33:3 says, "Call unto me, and I will answer thee." It is a sin not to pray. 1 Samuel 12:23 says, "Moreover as for me, God forbid that I should sin against the Lord in ceasing to pray for you."

People get saved and grow closer to the Lord when we pray. Families, relatives, friends, coworkers. You can't talk to someone about the Lord until you first talk to the Lord about that someone. Prayer is vital. We need to be sensitive to the people around us. Someone prayed for you that you might be saved and that you might come to know the Lord as your personal Savior. All vital praying drains you of your vitality. It's what we call getting on your face before God and praying fervently before God for some request that you would like Him to consider. Maybe some person — perhaps even you — is going through a lot of trouble (sickness or illness). When was the last time you were on your face before God? To intercede is a sacrifice. We must take time to pray.

FACT 6 – Prayer is warfare.

Prayer is not bias reverie or tender, sweet words. It is spiritual warfare. If you are a prayer warrior, you know what I am talking about. Ephesians 6:12 says, "For we wrestle not against flesh and blood, but against principalities, against powers, against the rulers of the darkness of this world, against spiritual wickedness in high places." Why do I have trouble praying? Why can't I find time to pray? Listen, if the devil can keep you from praying, he can keep you weak in the faith. He doesn't care how many sermons are preached, how many evangelistic meetings we hold, how many Sunday school lessons are taught, or how many songs are sung. As long as he can keep you from praying he has you where he wants you. Defeated.

We need to come boldly before the throne of grace. Hebrews 4:16 says, "Let us therefore come boldly unto the throne of grace, that we may obtain mercy, and find grace to help in time of need." When Christ was crucified on the Cross, the veil in the temple that separated the Most Holy Place from the Holy Place was torn in two. Only once every year could the high priest go into the Most Holy Place. If at any time someone touched that veil, they were struck dead immediately. When Christ died on the Cross of Calvary, the veil was torn in two from the top to the bottom allowing every person who prays to God to come into the Holy of Holies. Boldly.

We need to pray with authority. Ephesians 6:18 says, "Praying always with all prayer and supplication and watching there unto with all perseverance and supplication for all saints." Supplication is to pray humbly and earnestly with serious intention, with a sincere heart and a sober mind. Perseverance is to be persistent and steadfast, continuing in prayer despite the difficulties. There is no way to rebuke the devil without authority from God. The authority we have is our righteousness and privilege as children of God, which gives us freedom and access by prayer into the very throne room of God (Ephesians 3:12). The devil is like a roaring lion (1 Peter 5:8), but greater is He that is in us than he that is in the world (1 John 4:4).

FACT 7 – Prayer is worship.

Did you know nothing is impossible for God? There isn't anything He cannot do because He is the all-powerful, all-knowing, all-seeing, all-loving, all-wise God. Prayer is worship. Matthew 6:9 says pray in the name of the Lord and "Hallowed be Thy name." That is worship. "Hallowed be Thy name" means to set God apart. It means to honor Him. It means to revere Him, to esteem Him above all others.

He inhabits eternity; He sits in the most high and holy place. He rides the wings of the wind. His majesty is written across the sky. Through prayer, our petitions and our requests should be hedged on either side by worship. We start with worship, and we end with worship. This is heavenly etiquette. This is following the specifications, the instructions. We need to learn that prayer is not plunging in and making requests, but it is worshipping God, giving Him the due respect required of us as His children. When we come to God in prayer, the one who is the fountain of all things, His name is hallowed. He is the Lord your God. He is your protector. He supplies your every need. He is your peace, your strength, your righteousness, your salvation. He is always there; that is what His name represents. He is your "Father which art in Heaven, Hallowed be His name (Matthew 6:9).

If I hallow the name of God, set Him apart, honor Him, give Him all the praise and all the glory, revere Him, and hold Him above all others, I have a deep sense and awareness of who He is. And I acknowledge that. Christianity doesn't begin with man. It begins with God.

I will close with these verses. Hebrews 4:14-16 says, "Seeing then that we have a great high priest, that is past into the heavens, Jesus the Son of God, let us hold fast to our profession. For we have not an high priest which cannot be touched with the feeling of our infirmities; but was in all points tempted like as we are, yet without sin. Let us therefore come boldly unto the throne of grace, that we might obtain mercy, and find grace to help in time of need." What an encouragement this is!

Prayer is the only thing that is going to move the hand of God in your life, in your family's lives, in church, in this nation, in this world. May God bless you. May God encourage you and build you up in the most holiest of faiths, and may our God challenge you to a deeper prayer life.

CHAPTER 12 | FACTS 78-84

7 Defenses of
The Christian

"And He laid hold on the dragon, that old serpent, which is the devil, and Satan, and bound him a thousand years" (Revelation 20:2). That old serpent who deceived Adam and Eve into rebelling against the Word of God is none other than the devil or Satan. He's often viewed in Scripture as a great dragon. His ultimate doom is sure. He will be bound for 1,000 years, then finally cast into the Lake of Fire where he will be tormented day and night forever and ever (Revelation 20:10).

At present, however, he is not bound. "Your adversary the devil, as a roaring lion, walketh about, seeking whom he may devour" (1 Peter 5:8). And Paul goes on to tell us that we must be sober and vigilant that Satan should not get an advantage over us, for we are not ignorant of his devices. We all know when we are being tempted by Satan. The Apostle Paul tells us that we should not be ignorant of his devices that he uses to tempt us, for every one of us is tempted in a different way.

His devices are many, but all are deceptive. He is the most subtle of all God's creatures. His goal, his purpose is to turn us away from the true Christ. Again the Apostle Paul tells us in 2 Corinthians 11:3, "But I fear, lest by any means, as the serpent beguiled Eve through his subtilty, so your minds should be corrupted from the simplicity that is in Christ." Many people tell us that biblical salvation is too simple. They like to make it harder. The devil likes to make it different. He likes to make us think we can obtain salvation by works of righteousness, which we have done instead of by the works of righteousness, which Christ has done. He is always trying to deceive us that this simplicity of biblical salvation is not really true.

He is a great deceiver. He can appear as a fire-breathing dragon or a roaring lion, deceiving us into fearing and obeying him instead of God. He can also be transformed into an angel of light, deceiving us into trusting the words of false teachers instead of the Holy Scriptures of the God of Creation. Our recourse against his deception is to put on the whole armor of God that we may be able to stand against the wiles of the devil (Ephesians 6:11).

In this chapter I want to look at Ephesians 6 beginning in verse 11, "Put on the whole armour of God, that ye may be able to stand against the wiles of the devil. For we wrestle not against flesh and blood, but against principalities, against powers, against the rulers of the darkness of this world, against spiritual wickedness in high places. Wherefore take unto you the whole armour of God, that ye may be able to withstand in the evil day, and having done all, to stand."

There are many military metaphors in Scripture but none more famous than this passage on the armor of God. The Scripture likens a Christian to a soldier ready for battle. We are commanded to put on the whole armor, so we can stand, that is to be firm or well established, against the wiles of the devil. In this passage we find seven pieces of armor to put on, and we find each piece is crucial.

DEFENSE 1 – Belt of truth.

The first piece of armor is found in Ephesians 6:14: "Stand therefore, having your loins girt about with truth." The girdle, or low body armor, was designed to protect from wounds, which though not fatal, would cause great pain and incapacity. Truth is your protection against Satan's lie. He is a liar, and there is no truth in him. Satan's strength is in non-truth, which he uses to deceive the whole world when he comes at us and says, "Are you sure?" "Are you sure the Bible is true? Are you sure Jesus is the way to Heaven?" We can be spoiled by philosophy. We can be beguiled by good-sounding words. We can be tossed to and fro by other doctrine. We can even depart from the faith by listening to seducing spirits. Never before in the history of this world do we need people to stand for the truth. Christians need to walk in the truth and let their deeds be made manifest by doing the truth.

DEFENSE 2 – Breastplate of righteousness.

Our second piece of armor is found in this same verse, Ephesians 6:14, where it says "And having on the breastplate of righteousness." The stand that the Christian is expected to make against the principalities and powers of wickedness is made possible by the protection provided by this great breastplate of righteousness. This is the strong upper body armor designed to ward off the fatal blows of the enemy to our vital organs. The moment you are saved, you are justified — in other words, "just as if I never sinned" in the eyes of God. God imputes, or He places to your account, the righteousness of the Lord Jesus Christ. He also pronounces you righteous, and He treats you as a righteous person. As soldiers engaged in active warfare, we are to put on righteousness as a breastplate. We are to follow after righteousness (1 Timothy 6:11). We are to separate ourselves from unclean things. We are to yield our bodies as instruments of righteousness to God (Romans 6:13). We are to awake to righteousness and sin not (1 Corinthians 15:34). According to Romans 3:22, the Lord's righteousness has come upon those who believe. This lifestyle of righteousness now is the Christians' assurance that the Lord will bless and defend us in the battle. With God's righteousness we can go in the strength of the Lord God, and in His righteousness we shall be exalted. If you have accepted Christ as your Savior, you are now a righteous person. The Bible tells us that the Lord's eyes are upon the righteous, and His ears are open to their prayers. Jesus said in Matthew 25:46 that the righteous will go into eternal life.

DEFENSE 3 – Feet shod with the preparation of the Gospel of peace.

The third piece of armor is found in Ephesians 6:15: "And your feet shod with the preparation of the Gospel of peace." Shoes don't sound like an important part in this armor of God, yet they play a vital part in the effective warfare of a Christian. They are defined as the preparation of the Gospel with the emphasis on preparation. The Gospel is the good news about the death, burial, and resurrection of the Lord Jesus Christ. No Gospel would be clear without the presentation of sin and its awful consequences for the unbeliever. People need to know they are sinners, and they are sinners by nature. Sin is a natural part of our lives. Peter tells us that we must always be ready to give an answer to every man of the hope that is within us (1 Peter 3:15). The Apostle Paul also tells us that he was set for the defense of the gospel (Philippians 1:17). We are to know how to answer every man (1 Peter

3:15). Defending the Gospel against the attacks of Satan is the Christian's responsibility. This great work cannot be carried out by the wisdom of words. Our feet must be shod with the solid preparation of the Gospel. Then we will not suffer injury, and we can run and not be weary and walk and not faint.

DEFENSE 4 – Shield of faith.

The fourth piece of armor is found in Ephesians 6:16: "Above all, taking the shield of faith, wherewith ye shall be able to quench all the fiery darts of the wicked." Of the elements of the defensive pieces of God's armor for the Christian, the shield of faith is so important that it's said to be "above all." Perhaps this is because it is to be used to quench all the fiery darts of the wicked. In Paul's day the armament or the weapons were different. Armies had thousands and thousands of bowmen. These were men who would shoot bows and arrows. The arrows were the most important offensive weapon in a battle. In Paul's day, this is how armies would fight: One army would surround another army and get that army in the center. Then these bowmen, thousands and thousands of them, would dip their arrowheads into oil and set them ablaze. Then all these thousands of bowmen would shoot these arrows into the air into the center of this army they had surrounded. These flaming arrows were designed to create fear and to set fires within the camp, thus dividing and driving the soldiers away from their ranks into unprotected, open areas where they could be captured. It worked unless the shield was used. As these great volleys of arrows would come, thousands and thousands at a time, the sky was ablaze with the hiss and sizzle of these flaming arrows. The only effective defense against this flaming barrage was for all the soldiers to form ranks together and raise their shields joining themselves side by side, foot to foot, arm to arm, shoulder to shoulder. They would raise their shields to form a roof of shields over them, thus protecting themselves from these flaming arrows. The shield was their only defense. It's a shield of faith.

How do we get faith? Do we get faith by living a good life for Christ? Do we get faith by going to church or Sunday school? No. Romans 10:17 says, "So then faith cometh by hearing, and hearing by the Word of God." The way we can get faith and more faith is to read the Word of God. There are different levels of reading the Word of God. Some people feel they get enough of the Word of God just by coming to church and hearing the preacher preach the Word. Or they come to a Sunday school class and hear the Sunday school teacher teach the Word. Other people feel maybe if they read one verse in the morning, they get enough of the Word of God. These are various stages. God would have us to study the Word as the Bible commands us. I know everybody cannot take time to read a Bible commentary or sit down and read 10 chapters of the Bible every day. But the point here is we need to begin to study the Word, not only read the Word. The more you study the Word of God, the more the Word gets hold of you, and the more you can write the Word of God on the tables of your heart. Satan will flee if we resist and are steadfast in the faith. We use the Word of God when we are being tempted by Satan. I usually say these words, "Get thee behind me Satan, for the Lord God is within me. For greater is He that is in me than you that are in the world. So get away from me. Don't tempt me." You know I found out many, many times, Satan will leave me if I begin to quote the Word of God. I can ward off these fiery darts that he consistently and continually hails against me. You can too.

DEFENSE 5 – Helmet of salvation.

The fifth piece of armor is found in Ephesians 6:17, "And take the helmet of salvation." In the armor of the Christian soldier, none is as indispensable as the helmet of salvation. Many soldiers have fought on after terrible and hurtful wounds to their bodies, but a blow to the head renders one either insensible, unconscious, or dead. God mentioned this in Genesis 3:15 when He told the devil that the devil would bruise the heel of the Lord Jesus Christ, but Christ would bruise his head. Not only does the helmet protect us from fatal blows from the enemy, but it inspires us and encourages us with confidence to take part in the battle. No soldier would ever fight without his helmet. If I were not saved, I would not be in this battle, nor would I be concerned about its outcome. Many religious leaders today want us to put on the helmet of works of righteousness we have done, or to fill our minds with the vain philosophy of men. But as we have put our faith in the Lord Jesus Christ, we have been made wise to the Gospel, which is the power of God unto salvation. We have been protected and encouraged through the helmet of our salvation to proclaim it.

DEFENSE 6 – Sword of the Spirit.

The sixth piece of armor is found in Ephesians 6:17: "And take the helmet of salvation, and the sword of the Spirit, which is the Word of God." In this battle that we are expected to wage against the powers of this world, only one attack weapon is given to us. It is here identified as the Word of God. This great sword, which is quick and powerful, is to be that by which we live. This weapon is mighty. It is so sharp it penetrates "even to the dividing asunder of soul and spirit, and of the joints and marrow, and is a discerner of the thoughts and intents of the heart" (Hebrews 4:12). Praise God, with such a weapon we can't lose unless we keep it in the scabbard. The Greek term used here for *word* is *rema*, which means *the spoken word*. In this warfare in which we must stand and fight, our weapon is the spoken word. The great truths of God do no good sheathed between the covers of our

Bibles. As Christians we need to take out our sword, open our mouths, and proclaim the Gospel to a lost and dying world. You see, we may be the only Bible the world ever reads or hears. We who know the need must sow the seed.

DEFENSE 7 – Praying always.

Our last piece of armor is found in Ephesians 6:18, "Praying always with all prayer and supplication in the Spirit, and watching thereunto with all perseverance and supplication for all saints." As soldiers in this battle, we always need to be in communication with our commander. Poor communication could mean defeat. The first thing an army establishes in warfare is a good network of communication. Those on the front lines need direction from their commander about the battle plan. Prayer is invited. God says, "Call on me" (Psalm 50:15). He says let your requests be made known unto him (Philippians 4:6). Prayer is essential. Nothing gets done right without prayer. It is also specific. When you pray, you need to pray for specifics. Prayer is persistent. We need to "continue in prayer" (Colossians 4:2). It is also vital. The only thing that moves the hand of God is prayer. Prayer is warfare. We wrestle not against flesh and blood but against spiritual wickedness in high places (Ephesians 6:12), and prayer is worship. We need to hallow the name of God in prayer (Matthew 6:9). In other words, that means to set Him apart from everything and anything we know here on earth. We need Him to be the most special person in our lives. We need to set Him apart from everything and acknowledge Him as our Father in Heaven. As we put on this armor of God, it will help us to be more effective as Christians. It will help us to be more steadfast and victorious to overcome the world and live a life pleasing to our Lord.

CHAPTER 13 | FACTS 85-91

7 Facts About
The Rapture of the Church

In this chapter I would like to talk about the Rapture. In Revelation 4:1, the Apostle John said, "After this…" After what? "This" refers to what John just spoke about in Revelation 2 and 3. These letters were a spiritual outline of the Church Age from Pentecost until the Rapture. In Revelation 4:1 we see these words: "Come up hither."

Five people in Scripture have been translated up into Heaven while still having a physical body. The first was Enoch in Genesis 5:24. The second one was Elijah in 2 Kings 2:11. The third was the Lord Jesus Christ in Luke 24:51. The Apostle Paul in 2 Corinthians 12:2 was called up into the third Heaven, and John in Revelation 4 was called by Jesus to "Come up hither."

This statement of "Come up hither" is a symbol or representation of the Rapture. Among the 774,744 words in the Bible, the word *Rapture* cannot be found. But neither can the words *trinity* or *Bible* or *grandfather*. But there is a trinity, and Bibles and grandfathers do exist. The word *Rapture* comes from the Latin word *rapia* and the Greek word *harpazo*. They mean *called up* or *to catch away*. The word *Rapture* implies that something is taken with an irresistible force and moved rapidly and suddenly to another location. It signifies both a *carrying away* and *a blissful experience*.

The first mention or hint of a Rapture is found in John 14:2-3 where Jesus says, "In my Father's house are many mansions: if it were not so, I would have told you. I go to prepare a place for you. And if I go and prepare a place for you, I will come again, and receive you unto myself; that where I am, there ye may be also." The Rapture is not the Second Coming of Christ. The Rapture and the Second Coming of Christ are seven years apart. At the Rapture Christ comes in the air. At the Second Coming, Christ comes to the earth. At the Rapture He comes *for* His saints. At His Second Coming He comes *with* His saints. The timing of the Rapture we do not know. The timing of His Second Coming we do know. It is right after the Tribulation period.

The Rapture is the blessed hope of the church; as believers we are supposed to be looking for this glorious event (Titus 2:10-14). At the Second Coming Jesus Christ comes for judgment. The Rapture takes place in a moment. He comes as a thief in the night. At the Second Coming the whole world will see Him (Matthew 24:27-31).

Two Scripture passages describe this glorious event known as the Rapture. The first passage is 1 Corinthians 15:51-53, and the second one is 1 Thessalonians 4:13-18.

To me the 1 Thessalonians passage is the most thrilling passage in the Bible! It is the most encouraging passage of Scripture to the believer concerning the Rapture. In 1 Thessalonians 4:13-18 Paul says, "But I would not have you to be ignorant, brethren, concerning them which are asleep, that ye sorrow not, even as others which have no hope. For if we believe that Jesus died and rose again, even so them also which sleep in Jesus will God bring with him. For this we say unto you by the Word of the Lord, that we which are alive and remain unto the coming of the Lord shall not prevent them which are asleep. For the Lord himself shall descend from Heaven with a shout, with the voice of the archangel, and with the trump of God: and the dead in Christ shall rise first: Then we which are alive and remain shall be caught up together with them in the clouds, to meet the Lord in the air: and so shall we ever be with the Lord. Wherefore comfort one another with these words."

In verse 13 Paul uses the word *ignorant*. He is not being rude. He is just saying he does not want you to be unlearned about the Rapture. The Apostle Paul uses this word *ignorant* in four other passages of Scripture. In 1 Corinthians 10:1, he is talking about the events in the Old Testament when God led the children of Israel as they left captivity in Egypt. He led them out of Egypt and through the Red Sea to the Promised Land. God does not want His people — or us — to be ignorant about that very fact. Another place he uses the word is in Romans 11:25 when Paul is discussing Jesus bringing restoration to Israel. Right now, during this Age of Grace, blindness has come to Israel. Israel does not believe that Jesus Christ was its Messiah; so therefore, during this age Israel has been sidetracked. But a time is coming when all of Israel will accept Jesus Christ as its Messiah and personal Savior. Israel will be restored to God (Romans 11:26). In 1 Corinthians 12 (this is concerning spiritual gifts), Paul says he does not want us to be ignorant about the fact that there are temporal and permanent spiritual gifts. Some of these temporal spiritual gifts such as speaking in tongues, interpreting tongues, raising people from the dead, and healing people miraculously were evident during what is known as the Apostolic Church Age. This was the first 100 years after Christ's death on the Cross of Calvary when God was bringing forth the New Testament by inspiration. He gave this power of these marvelous gifts to the apostles, but this power was temporal. When we received the Scriptures, those gifts were done away with. *Katargeo* in the Greek means *they shall cease.* There are permanent gifts for this day and age, and Paul does not want us to be ignorant about this very fact. The other place where Paul uses the word *ignorant* is found in Acts 17:30 concerning salvation; God would have all men to repent and be saved.

I want to share seven facts about the Rapture with you.

FACT 1 – The Rapture is a mystery.

In 1 Corinthians 15:51 Paul is writing to the Corinthian church, and he states, "Behold..." The word *behold* is an exciting word. It is a word that you need to notice. Paul is saying, "BEHOLD, I want to tell you something here. I show you a mystery." This is one of 11 mysteries in the Bible. We have the mystery of the church, the mystery of iniquity, the mystery of Babylon and so forth. What is the mystery or secret concerning the Rapture?

A mystery in Scripture is a previously hidden truth, and now it is divinely revealed by God. Suppose you began reading the Bible, and you started in Genesis 1 and read through to 1 Corinthians 14. If you stopped your reading at 1 Corinthians 14, you would have learned a great deal. You would have learned about creation, about the flood, and about man's sin. You would have learned about Calvary, but you would be forced to conclude that Christians can only get to Heaven through physical death. But in 1 Corinthians 15, the secret is out. Here it is: Millions of Christians someday will reach Heaven without dying. "Behold, I show you a mystery; We shall not all die." This is the mystery of the Rapture.

FACT 2 – The Lord will descend from his throne in Heaven.

The Lord Himself (no angel, no group of angels, no other heavenly beings) will descend. It will be literal, physical, and visible. He will descend from Heaven. Jesus is in Heaven. He is not in the grave. He is resurrected. He ascended up to Heaven after His resurrection (Luke 24:51). He is our living Savior seated at the right hand of God the Father and is our advocate, our mediator, and our intercessor. He represents us before the throne of God, and He is coming from His throne in Glory.

He is coming for every believer. We are His personal possession. We will be his bride. During this Age of Grace the church is engaged to the Lord Jesus Christ. This is one of the seven blessings of being saved. We were sealed by the Holy Spirit. We were adopted into the family of God, and we are children of the King. The King is coming for us!

FACT 3 – Jesus will descend with a shout, with the voice of the archangel, and the sound of trumpets.

Jesus will descend with a shout. It will be the same shout that He used when He called Lazarus from the dead (John 11). Jesus will shout, "Come up hither." It will be a shout that all Christians both living and dead will hear. A day is coming when all those who are in the grave will hear His voice and come forth (John 5:28-29).

Paul states in 1 Corinthians 15:52 that the last trump will sound. This will be His last call. It is the voice of the Lord Jesus Christ Himself. He is going to call all believers, living and dead, to come forth. This will be His last call to Heaven. It's known as the first resurrection. The first resurrection refers to the resurrection of those who have received Christ as their Savior. This first resurrection is in three segments. If you recall in the New Testament when Jesus Christ was crucified, many people were resurrected out of the grave. All of those who have died (believers that is) from the Cross until the Rapture occurs will be in the first resurrection. Then there will be the Tribulation saints. These are the ones who got saved by the preaching of the 144,000 Jewish preachers (Revelation 7) and were martyred for the cause of Christ during the Tribulation (Revelation 20:4). Their bodies will also be resurrected in the first resurrection. The bodies of all the Old Testament saints from the time of Adam until the time of the Cross will be resurrected. All of those people who received Christ as their Savior, their bodies are in the grave and will be resurrected. All of these segments of resurrection make up the first resurrection (Revelation 20:5-6), over which the second death has no power. At this time (the time we are living in right now), He is softly and tenderly calling the sinner to repentance. His call has been continuous throughout this Age of Grace. For He would have all men saved and come to the knowledge of the truth.

2 Peter 3:9 tells us "the Lord is not slack concerning His promise" of His coming, but He is long-suffering, "not willing that any should perish, but that all should come to repentance." A day is coming when time will be no more. The last call will be given, and for those who have rejected His call during the Age of Grace, there will be no more calling. There will be no second chance for people who lived in this Age of Grace and rejected Jesus Christ as their Savior to ever receive Christ as their Savior during the Tribulation time.

Both of these passages on the Rapture, 1 Corinthians 15 and 1 Thessalonians 4, talk about trumpets. Fifty-one verses in the Bible refer to trumpets. In the Old Testament the trumpet was used for two things. One was to summon to battle. For instance, we read in the Old Testament when Joshua fought the battle of Jericho, the trumpets were sounded to battle. The second time trumpets were sounded was a call to worship. The priests would blow the trumpets, and all the people of Israel would assemble themselves at the door of the Tabernacle.

To the angels at the time of the Rapture, the trumpet blast will mean *prepare for battle*. Michael the Archangel, will lead a heavenly host of angels to fight against the devil and his demons to clear the air. Remember the devil is the prince and power of the air around the earth, and Michael is going to clear the air for the coming of the Lord Jesus Christ. The trump of God will sound as Jesus descends. The sound of trumpets will echo and reverberate through the canyons of clouds for all saved people to hear. To the believers living and dead, the call will be to worship. Prepare to meet our Savior and Lord in the air! We will hear the sounding of these trumpets as the voice of Christ calls us to "Come up hither."

The voice of the archangel also will be part of the Rapture. Enumerable angels are in Heaven, and there are classes of angels. There are seraphim and cherubim, and there are archangels. The archangels seem to be the highest class of angels. Michael is one of them; Gabriel is another. The one at the Rapture will be Michael. Michael is associated with resurrections.

FACT 4 – The dead in Christ will rise first in an incorruptible form.

The dead in Christ will rise first. The dead in Christ are the believers from the time of the Cross until the Rapture takes place, who have suffered physical death and are all waiting for this glorious and blessed event. Their corruptible bodies that have been in the grave, some for 2,000 years, will be brought together in an incorruptible body to be united with their soul and spirit in the air.

When a person suffers physical death, their soul and their spirit go to Heaven, and their bodies go into the grave. We are trichotomous. We have three distinct features, which make us different from plants and animals. We have a body, a soul, and a spirit (1 Thessalonians 5:23). The body houses the soul and the spirit. The soul is the seat of our emotion, our reasoning, our intellect. The spirit makes us God conscious. These bodies will rise first to be reunited with their soul and their spirit.

The dead will be raised incorruptible. Right now we live in a corruptible body; one that was created from the dust of the earth and is subject to death. "It is appointed unto men once to die" (Hebrews 9:27). When the believer dies in the Lord, his soul and spirit go to Heaven, but his body goes into the grave to a corruptible state and turns back to dust. But when the voice of the Lord is heard and the trumpets are sounded, that corruptible body that is in the grave is going to be raised incorruptible. It will be changed never to die again. A day is coming when all believers who are in the grave will hear His voice and be raised to newness of life.

FACT 5 – Those who are alive in Christ will be called up together with those who were dead.

1 Thessalonians 4:17 says, "Then we which are alive and remain shall be caught up." The "we" is the same "we" as in verse 14 of the same chapter. This is the existing church, the *ecklesia*, the *called out ones*. It is all of us who have received and believed in Jesus Christ as our personal Savior, who are alive at the time of the Rapture. Every living believer, alive physically and spiritually, who is living on the earth at this time is included. Red and yellow, black and white. All kindred, all nations and all tongues. The living believers who remain on earth will be held for a fraction of a moment to allow the dead bodies to rise out of the grave first.

This is your loved ones, your spouse, your children, your grandchildren, families, relatives, friends, your church congregation. I thank God by His grace that my wife and all of my children are saved.

FACT 6 – We will all be changed in a moment, and this mortal will put on immortality.

The next fact I want to look at is we will all be changed. We will be changed and ready for the transition from this old earth. We will be called up — Raptured. We will suddenly and rapidly be relocated by an irresistible force to a new location called Heaven.

"We" and "all" are referring to all the living and dead believers in Christ. Someday a miraculous change will take place, a supernatural transformation. We will all be changed and made ready to meet the King of Kings and Lord of Lords, our Savior.

Paul goes on to say in 1 Corinthians 15:52, "In a moment…" This great change, when it finally occurs, will take place in a moment. The Greek word is *en-atomo* — *in an atom of time*. This word *atom* implies in the Greek *the smallest particle of time*. It is used only this one time in the New Testament. This happening is further described by the twinkling of an eye. How long is that? Well, it's in a moment. We won't even have time to say, "Here He comes!" People who study time tell us it is 1/10,000 of a second. I can't understand that speed. I do know that when He appears, we will be like Him; for we will see Him as He is in that very moment.

1 Corinthians 15:54 says this mortal must put on immortality. Right now we live in a mortal body subject to sickness and disease, pain and suffering, tensions and stress, and death itself. But when we put on immortality, the Lord Jesus Christ will instantly give us new bodies. Our new bodies will be like Christ's resurrected body. Philippians 3:21 says, "Who shall change our vile body, that it may be fashioned like unto His glorious body, according to the working whereby he is able even to subdue all things unto Himself."

Christ is able to create new bodies for us in a moment just as when He created all things in the beginning. When He spoke, it was done. Creation is a visible testimony to the power of God and the great things He can do. The Lord is great and greatly to be praised (Psalm 48:1). His greatness endures forever.

FACT 7 – We will meet the Lord in the air and be with Him forever.

We are going to be called up with the previously dead believers to meet the Lord. We've read about Him, we've talked about Him, we've learned about Him, and we've sung about Him. Finally we are going to meet Him. Oh yes! Face to face in all of His glory!

We will ever and always be with the Lord Jesus Christ. We will never leave Him. We will never be separated from Him, nor will He ever leave or forsake us. We will be with Him throughout all the ages of eternity; that is forever and ever. 1 Thessalonians 4:18 says, "Wherefore comfort (or exhort) one another with these words."

Whatever you do, don't miss this!

CHAPTER 14 | **FACTS 92-98**

7 Signs of
The End Times

During Jesus' ministry here on earth, He often told His disciples that He was going to be crucified, and He also talked about the end of the world. During the crucifixion week the disciples came to Jesus at the Mount of Olives, and they asked Him when these things were going to happen. What will be the sign of His coming and the end of the world? (Matthew 24:3)

There is an increasing, overwhelming desire among many people to know about the end times. Many people believe the end of the world will occur with the earth being blown up such as by atomic bomb, and that will be the end. They are anxious, some worried, and many confused. They are attending all kinds of prophecy conferences, and many of these are not Scripturally based. I think our inquisitive nature wants to know how much time is left. Where are we on God's timetable? Can we still believe that Jesus is coming? Are the signs of the time occurring today?

Are we the generation of the Rapture? What will happen when Jesus comes? These are all valid questions.

Since the rebirth of the nation of Israel in 1948, Christians have had a growing awareness that God's timetable has been moving toward the end times. Dr. John Walvord, one of the world's foremost prophetic scholars, said, "Never before in history, have all the factors been present for the fulfillment of prophecy relating to the end times. Only in our generation have the combined revival of Israel, the push toward a one-world church, the increasing power of Islam, the rise of the occults worldwide, spread of atheistic philosophy all been present at one time. The road to Armageddon is already mapped and being paved."

Since the Bible sets no dates or time limits on the completion of prophecy, we are all left guessing how close we are to the end. Mark 13:32 tells us that neither man nor angels can know the exact time when Christ will come again. The timing of the last days is in God's hand. The pieces of the puzzle are all in place. I believe Jesus could come at any moment. Nothing scripturally has to take place. No red heifer has to be found. No red heifer ashes need to be used. No temple has to be built. No Ark of the Covenant has to be found. All that needs to happen has happened. Jesus could come at any moment. As the sands of time slip through God's hourglass, we are moving closer to an appointment with eternity.

We as Christians are to be anticipating this magnificent event. In other words, we are to be looking earnestly for the Lord to come. The Christian is faced with a dilemma. The tension between living for today and looking for tomorrow is one of the realities of the Christian's life in this day and age. On one hand, we need to be ready for Jesus to come at any moment. On the other hand, we have God-given responsibilities to fulfill in this world in the meantime until Jesus comes for us. We need to keep on keeping on and looking for His coming.

Here are seven facts of the end times. Matthew 16:2 tells us, "When it is evening, ye say, It will be fair weather: for the sky is red." This reminds me of the saying, "Red skies at night are a sailor's delight, and red skies in the morning are a sailor's warning." Are we given any signs or indications that the last days are upon us? We certainly are! Jesus Himself said in Matthew 24:33, "When ye shall see all these things, know that it is near, even at the doors."

SIGN 1 – An increase in wars and rumors of wars.

In Matthew 24:6, Jesus warned of continual wars. In the past 78 years, we have had two World Wars and a countless number of other wars and conflicts, which continue even to this very day. We are faced with the War on Terror; we have been at war in Iraq and in Afghanistan. There is also a threat of war in the Middle East and a war with North Korea. The increase of wars and rumors of war continues to this day. War seems to be the solution to man's problem with mankind.

SIGN 2 – Extreme materialism.

2 Timothy 3:1-2 says, "This know also, that in the last days perilous times shall come. For men shall be lovers of their own selves." In the last days men will be lovers of themselves and be covetous. When have you ever known or read in history books of a time when there has been as much materialism as there is today? In America, we want for nothing, and if we want something badly enough, we get it. This desire for material things is spreading all over the world. We have a name for this. We call it the "quality of life." It is a desire to have everything we want at any cost.

SIGN 3 – Lawlessness.

The third sign, found in 2 Timothy 3, is lawlessness. As the Apostle Paul continues in verses 2-4, men will be "boasters, proud, blasphemers, disobedient to parents, unthankful, unholy, without natural affection, truce breakers, false accusers, incontinent, fierce, despisers of those that are good, traitors, heady, high minded." These words describe to a tee the days we are living in, and it will continue until the Tribulation when there will be total chaos, pandemonium, and rebellion throughout all of the earth. Let's look at these words in 2 Timothy 3.

1. Boaster means to brag about oneself.
2. Proud is showing oneself esteemed, being arrogant.
3. Blasphemers speak profanity of God, to curse His name.
4. Disobedience is a refusal to obey.
5. Unthankful is unappreciative, ungrateful.
6. Unholy is disrespect for God, spiritually impure, and without natural affection. This is the gay lifestyle that is sweeping the world.
7. Truce breakers are disloyal and dishonest.
8. False accusers are those who accuse you falsely for the right things you do.
9. Incontinent is no sexual restraint, sexual promiscuity.
10. Fierce is to be violent, lawless, no respect or concern for the rights of others.
11. Despisers dislike you for the good things you do.
12. Traitors are ones who betray your trust.
13. Haughty is to be intoxicating, headstrong.
14. High minded is to be puffed up, conceited, thinking only of oneself. Lovers of pleasure rather than lovers of God.

SIGN 4 – An Increase in speed and knowledge.

Daniel 12:4 tells us at the end times "many shall run to and fro, and knowledge shall be increased." After reading this, the great Christian and scientist Sir Isaac Newton said, "Personally, I believe in the end times, man will travel from country to country in an unprecedented manner. There may be inventions that will enable man to travel at and perhaps exceed 50 miles per hour." Several years later the infamous French atheist Voltaire read Newton's words and retorted, "See what a fool Christianity makes out of a brilliant man like Newton. Why if a man would travel at 50 miles per hour, he would suffocate. His heart would stand still. His eyes would pop out on his cheeks." I wonder what Voltaire would say if he knew that on June 3, 1965, astronaut Ed White climbed out of a spacecraft 100 miles above the earth and walked across the United States — some 3,000 plus miles in 15 minutes traveling at the speed of 17,500 miles per hour. Travel began to increase in the 1960s with the jet age. Now millions of people travel the world over. They are going to and fro. They travel from here to there.

There is an increase of knowledge. We now have more than 60 million students in America alone who attend some 72,000 public elementary schools, 27,000 secondary schools, and 12,000 colleges and universities. Each year our government spends billions of dollars on education. This increase in knowledge started in 1960. Now most high school seniors go on to higher education. We are in the computer age and have the Internet; You can find anything you want to know on the Internet. We are "Ever learning, and never able to come to the knowledge of the truth (2 Timothy 3:7).

SIGN 5 – Departure from the Christian faith.

2 Thessalonians 2:3 talks about a time when there will be a great falling away from Christianity. 1 Timothy 4:1 says, "Now the Spirit speaketh expressly, that in the latter times some shall depart from the faith." In the last 50 years there has been a great falling away and a departing from the Christian faith. Great churches that once preached the Gospel no longer do so. They

no longer preach the book, the blood, and the blessed hope. The Bible is no longer considered the mandate for church doctrine. Jesus is no longer the way, the truth, and the life. It is pluralism. All religions lead to Heaven, they claim. Churches are no longer filled on a Sunday morning. Prayer meetings have become a thing of the past. People would rather discuss than be taught. They would rather be entertained than be preached to. Cults and other religions are springing up all over the world. Our churches are no longer standing for the Word of God and the testimony of Jesus Christ. Opinions are put up against knowledge. That is the reason for this book, *120 Bible Facts Anyone Can Know*. The Apostle Paul's sad prediction has been fulfilled down to the last letter when he wrote, "Having a form of godliness, but denying the power thereof" (2 Timothy 3:5).

Linked with this departure from the faith is the unification of this world's systems. The Antichrist will someday successfully unite the religious, political, and economic systems of this world. We have a push to this unification today with the National Council of Churches and the World Council of Churches, through the ecumenical movement that all faiths get together under the banner of love and unity. This is a move toward a one-world church. We also have the push toward a new world order, which is being spearheaded by the United Nations to produce a one-world government. Then there is the setting up of the European Common Market or the United States of Europe. This sets the stage for the revived Roman Empire that will be in power during the seven-year Tribulation. Then there is the one-world monetary system, the same currency being used because of international trade and travel as people go to and fro. Another area is skin implants, known as human microchip implants, that contain your history and all your records. The president of Debolt, a bank equipment manufacturer, recently stated, "You will soon be able to do anything that you do today without cash or credit cards simply through skin implants or invisible tattoos." Revelation 13:16-17 says, "And he causeth all, both small and great, rich and poor, free and bond, to receive a mark in the right hand, or in their foreheads: And that no man might buy or sell, save he that had the mark, or the name of the beast, or the number of his name."

SIGN 6 – The paralleling of the days of Noah.

In Matthew 24:37 Jesus said, "But as the days of Noah were, so shall also the coming of the Son of man be." No history books describe the days of Noah. You must look in Genesis 4, 5, and 6 and read about the Canaanite civilization (the civilization of Noah).

A number of things about this civilization: The people had no fear of God because of Cain's disobedience and rebellious nature. He was running away from God and did not fear God. They were city builders. We today continue to expand our cities because of the great population growth here on earth. They had more than one wife. It was an agricultural age. Since 1936, because of our hybridization in agriculture, we can produce eight times more on one acre than we could in 1936. It was a musical age. It was a steel age. Today most everything you see (buildings, cars, etc.) has some type of steel in it. There was no concern for human life. It was an age of materialism and lawlessness. It sounds like I am reading from our daily newspaper or watching the evening news on television.

SIGN 7 – The sign of the fig tree.

I believe the most significant sign is found in Matthew 24:32-33 concerning the fig tree. It reads, "Now learn a parable of the fig tree; When his branch is yet tender, and putteth forth leaves, ye know that summer is nigh: So likewise ye, when ye shall see all these things, know that it is near, even at the doors." The fig tree is a symbol of the nation of Israel. After Israel disobeyed and failed God, it was scattered among the nations. The land of Israel, for the most part, became a barren wasteland. The once-great Jewish life and heritage became a hatred and mockery to the world. Since the destruction of Jerusalem by the Roman General Titus in A.D. 70, the "fig tree" stopped blooming. There have been many important dates in history. In A.D. 324, Constantine, the Roman emperor, adopted Christianity as the state religion of Rome. In A.D. 476 the Roman Empire fell. In 1492, Columbus sailed the world and discovered the Americas. On July 4, 1776, the U.S. Declaration of Independence was signed, giving us our independence from England. On August 6, 1945, the first atomic bomb was dropped on Japan. On July 20, 1969, the first man walked on the moon. But I believe the most important and significant date in history (since the Cross) occurred at 4:30 p.m. on May 14, 1948. Israel officially became a nation again by the United Nations' vote to accept it as a nation. Since that day, the Jewish people, who were scattered all over the world, have been returning to Israel.

Four major trends are happening today in our lifetimes that are crucial to biblical prophecy. Israel and the Middle East are the key to the last days prophecy.

Aliya

The first trend is *Aliya*. It is a Jewish word for *going up* or you can say *immigration*. There are three Aliyas in Israel's history. The first one was when the Jewish people were placed in captivity in Egypt under Pharaoh, and Moses, the deliverer, came and delivered them out of captivity and took them to the land that God had promised them. They were going up to Jerusalem.

The second Aliya was after the Jewish people were taken into another captivity by the Babylonian Empire, and they were held there for 70 years. After the decree of Darius to allow the Jewish people to go back to Jerusalem to rebuild the temple and the city, Zerubbabel took 50,000 of the Jewish people and made an Aliya back to Jerusalem to rebuild the city. Because of their disobedience and unfaithfulness to God, God scattered them among all people from the one end of the earth even unto the other (Deuteronomy 28). In Ezekiel 34:13 God says, "And I will bring them out from the people, and gather them from the countries, I will bring them to their own land."

The third Aliya occurs in the last days as Israel establishes itself as a nation. Since 1948 this has been happening. We have had Operation Moses, Operation Solomon, and Wings of Eagles. There has been a great exodus to Israel, especially after World War II in 1945. The Jewish people are returning to their homeland, the land God gave them in Exodus 3:8.

Alignment

The second trend is alignment. For the first 2,000 years of earth's history, there were only Gentiles on the earth. The Jewish race started with the call of Abraham. In fact, Abraham was a Gentile and became the father of the Jewish people. Deuteronomy 7:6-8 says God chose the Jewish people, the fewest people on the earth at the time, because He loved them.

We read in Daniel 2 of the Gentile world powers that were going to come upon this earth. Daniel 11 talks about five personalities that will come to power. They are Ahasuerus, Alexander the Great, Antiochus the Great, Antiochus Epiphanes, and the fifth man to come to power at the time of the end, the little horn of Daniel, the Beast out of the sea of Revelation 13:1, the Antichrist.

He will not be revealed until the Rapture of the church occurs. According to Daniel 9 the Antichrist will confirm a peace treaty for seven years with Israel, and because of that peace treaty, he must defend Israel. We find that he leaves Rome and enters the Glorious Land, which is Israel, and sets up his government and capital in Jerusalem. We also read in that chapter that the kings of the north and south are ready to go to war with their Jewish neighbor, Israel.

The revived Roman Empire is about to take form through the infrastructure of the European Union, formed in 1998. After conquering Syria and Egypt, the Antichrist will head for Jerusalem. In Daniel 11:43 we read the Libyans and Ethiopians are after him. According to Ezekiel 38 Russia, Turkey, and Iran will form a coalition to go to war with Israel in the last days.

The war clouds are rising in the skies over the Holy Lands as nuclear tension between Israel and Iran intensifies every day. Zechariah 12:9 reads, "And it shall come to pass in that day (this is talking about the last days), that I will seek to destroy all the nations that come against Jerusalem. And I will pour upon the house of David, and upon the inhabitants of Jerusalem, the spirit of grace and of supplication: and they shall look upon me whom they have pierced, and they shall mourn for him, as one mourneth for his only son, and shall be in bitterness for him, as one that is in bitterness for his firstborn. In that day shall there be a great mourning in Jerusalem." If you read the text carefully, you will see that the people of Israel must be in the land. Zechariah also makes it clear that the Jewish people would be living in Jerusalem. Until the 1967 war, Jerusalem was a divided city, but since 1967, it has been united under Jewish control.

This is the prophesy of the Second Coming of our Lord to this earth as He touches down on the Mount of Olives, and the mount is split in two. Then He goes to Petra, where God has given the Jewish remnant a place of protection and refuge during the last 3 1/2 years of the Tribulation (Revelation 12). God reminds us of the special role the Jewish people continue to play in His end times plans because His covenant with the Jewish people has never ended. They are still His chosen people. The Apostle Paul writes in Romans 11:25-26, "For I would not, brethren, that ye should be ignorant of this mystery, lest ye should be wise in your own conceits; that blindness in part is happened to Israel, until the fullness of the Gentiles be come in. And so all Israel shall be saved: as it is written, There shall come out of Zion the Deliverer and shall turn away ungodliness from Jacob." Israelites were chosen for a fourfold ministry.

1. They were to witness to the unity of God in the midst of universal idolatry.
2. They were to illustrate to the nations the blessedness of serving the true God.
3. They were to receive, preserve, and transmit the Scriptures.
4. They were to produce, as to His humanity, the Messiah.

According to the prophets, Israel regathered from all nations, restored to her own land, and converted is yet to have her greatest earthly exhortation and glory.

Peace

The third trend is peace. We hear about having peace in the Middle East. The United States has tried to bring about that peace with the Camp David Accord under President Carter; the meetings between President Reagan and Egyptian President Anwar Sadat; the Oslow Accord with President Clinton, Israeli President Yitzhak Rabin and PLO Chairman Yasir Arafat; and the Jordanian-Israeli Peace Treaty. This agreement has never come to fruition, but there has been a cold peace. Someone needs to confirm this peace agreement. *Confirm* means *to strengthen* or *to give formal approval.* Again we read in Daniel 9:27, "He shall confirm the covenant…" This is the fifth personality of Daniel 11, the Antichrist. He is going to confirm this peace treaty with Israel during the Tribulation period, which will last for seven years.

Temple Fervor

The fourth trend is temple fervor. There have been a number of Jewish temples. We had the first temple or the tabernacle of Moses. Then we had Solomon's Temple, Zerubbabel Temple, and Herod's Temple. There will be the Tribulation temple, which will be the temple that will be rebuilt in Jerusalem probably on the Temple Mount where an Islamic temple, the Dome of the Rock, now stands. During the Tribulation, the Antichrist is going to allow Israel to build that temple and again have temple worship.

Three times daily, prayers are offered at the Wailing Wall in Jerusalem. "May our temple be rebuilt in this day here in the Holy City," they pray. In A.D. 70 Titus, the Roman general, destroyed the temple, and since that time there has been no Jewish temple built in Jerusalem on the Temple Mount. Since their Aliya, there has been a great desire by the Jewish people to rebuild the temple. They are ready to rebuild. In fact, they have on their computers the names of all Jewish men in the world who are qualified to be priests. Some 38,000 are needed: 24,000 priests, 6,000 officers and judges, 4,000 porters, and 4,000 to play the musical instruments. They have 24,000 marked already. The priestly garments are made and ready for the high priest to wear. The instruments for the temple are made and ready: the mizrach, the silver cup, the golden flask, the incense chalice, the silver shovel, the lottery box, the copper washbasin, the silver trumpet, the 10-string harps. A couple, Micah and Shushanna Howery, are from New York City. He is a carpenter. They went to Jerusalem and found a 10-string harp in a cave. It was the first harp found in more than 2,000 years. He made a 10-string harp, and he has now been commissioned to make 1,000 of them. These will be used by the 4,000 people, who will play the musical instruments in the temple rituals and sacrifices the Jewish people will be allowed to have during the first 3 ½ years of the seven years of Tribulation.

In fact, I understand that the architectural plans are already drawn for this temple to be built in Jerusalem. As an architect I know about drawing plans. I know about building buildings. Today many of our buildings are built in a prefabricated method. In other words, the pieces of the building are built somewhere in a factory to quality control, and they are shipped to the site and then the contractors assemble them. This is called a fast-track building program. Buildings can go up 10 times faster than they could by regular construction methods. It would be very easy to understand that this temple that will be built on the Temple Mount could easily be built in the first three months of the Tribulation. This prophecy in Daniel concerning the peace treaty with the Jews and allowing them to worship for seven years in their temple can very easily come about.

We read in 1 Thessalonians 4, Daniel 9:27, and Revelation 12:12-17 that in the middle of the Tribulation, the Antichrist will desecrate the temple. He will set himself up as God. He will stop Jewish worship. The last half of the Tribulation becomes known as Jacob's trouble as the devil is cast out of Heaven down to this earth. He begins to persecute the Jews for the last 3 1/2 years of the Tribulation.

At the end of the Tribulation as the Lord Jesus Christ comes from Heaven and the battle of Armageddon is fought, He touches down on the Mount of Olives and goes to Petra. The Jewish people are reconciled to Jesus Christ. They finally realize that He was their promised Messiah, and they accept Him as their Savior. Then He takes them from Petra through Bozra up to the Temple Mount through the Eastern Gate where He will then begin to judge the nations of the world and usher in what is known as the Millennium, the 1,000-year rule and reign of Christ here on this earth. A new temple will be built, which will be known as the millennial temple, where our Savior, the Lord Jesus Christ, will set up His government. We are ordinary people saved by His grace for an extraordinary future with our Lord.

CHAPTER 15 | **FACTS 99–105**

7 Facts About
The Tribulation

The age we live in right now, the Bible says, will end in judgment. This judgment is known as the Tribulation period. There are various names for the Tribulation: the Day of the Lord, the Day of God's Vengeance, the Times of Troubles as Never Such Was, the Time of the End, the Hour of His Judgment, the End of the World, and the Time of Jacob's Trouble.

The Great Tribulation will be greater in its effect on all creation, especially in the duration of pain and suffering that man will undergo, than any other time in all of history. In fact, Jesus said, "And except those days should be shortened, there should no flesh be saved" (Matthew 24:22). The people of the earth will try to commit suicide to be relieved of their torment. Judgment will not bring repentance. In fact, mankind will become more evil, manifesting wickedness without restraint. Remember the church is removed, so the Holy Spirit is removed, and the restrainer isn't here. The Holy Spirit is in Heaven with the church.

Man will be given over to a reprobate mind, or will be hopelessly sinful, which will express itself in the worship of demons, idolatry, murders, sorceries, fornication, and theft. Man will be defiant against the Lord God Almighty. Earth will be a living hell.

I want to give you seven facts about the Tribulation.

FACT 1 – The Tribulation will last seven years.

The seven years are the "70th week" of Daniel's prophecy. Daniel 9:27 describes the "70 weeks" of prophecy to be fulfilled on this earth. We know that one "week" equals seven years. The prophecy of Daniel was for the time of the Jewish people, who were being held in Babylon in captivity under Nebuchadnezzar. From the time that they were allowed to go back to Jerusalem to build the walls and the temple that Nebuchadnezzar and his army destroyed was 69 "weeks" or 483 years, as Daniel prophesied.

This prophecy came true. These 483 years have already occurred. It's recorded in the Bible and also recorded in secular history. The "69 weeks" of the 483 years were a time when the Jews were allowed to go back to Jerusalem and rebuild the walls and the temple and also covered the time until Jesus entered Jerusalem before He was crucified. So "69 weeks" have passed, and we know one more "week" is left to come. It's like a basketball game with one minute left, and the referee calls a time out.

Jesus entered Jerusalem on Palm Sunday, and that following week He was crucified on Friday. Since then, more than 2,000 years have passed. Nothing has happened yet. This could be because God is long-suffering, for He would have all men to be saved. Also the Bible talks about a ransom that needs to be paid for the life of Jesus Christ. I believe the buzzer is about ready to sound to resume and end the game.

Revelation has the seven years of Tribulation divided into three periods. The first period is 1,260 days or 42 months or 3 1/2 years. (The Bible year, according to Genesis, is 360 days.) After the first 3 1/2 years, there will be a short time in the middle, perhaps a couple of weeks (Revelation 12). It will be followed by the last 1,260 days or 42 months or 3 1/2 years, equaling Daniel's prophecy of one "week" or seven years, according to Revelation 12:6.

FACT 2 – The church (saved people or believers) from all over the world will not be here.

The book of Revelation has the Tribulation period starting in chapter 6 and continuing through chapter 18. In chapters 1 through 5, the church is mentioned 19 times, and Israel is mentioned three times. From chapter 6 (that's the beginning of the Tribulation) and continuing through chapter 18 (the ending of the Tribulation) the church is mentioned zero times, and Israel is mentioned 26 times. The reason for this is the church is not here. The Rapture of the church and the Second Coming of Christ to this earth bookend the seven-year Tribulation period.

1 Thessalonians 1:10 says, "And to wait for His Son from Heaven, whom He raised from the dead, even Jesus, who delivered us from the wrath to come." 1 Thessalonians 5:9 states, "For God hath not appointed us (that's believers) to wrath, but to obtain salvation by our Lord Jesus Christ." Revelation 6 starts the content on the Tribulation, and verse 17 states, "For the great day of his wrath is come." It continues to escalate in ferocity throughout the seven-year Tribulation. 1 Thessalonians 2:6-7 tells us the Holy Spirit is not here on the earth during the seven-year Tribulation period. John sees Him in Heaven in Revelation 4:5. The reason for this is He was given to the church and believers to guide and comfort them. The church is in Heaven, and so is the Holy Spirit. Revelation 3:10 says the church is saved from the hour of Tribulation (temptation) here on this earth.

FACT 3 – The Tribulation will be a time of God's judgment.

Throughout man's sinful history here on planet earth, he has been subjected to many great calamities. The first great calamity was the flood of Genesis. All people perished except for eight people. Population experts assume the population was 235 million people at that time. In 1340 to 1350, 25 million people in Asia and Europe died of the Black Plague. On Jan. 24, 1556, some 830,000 people died in China from a massive earthquake. In 1560, 3 million people died of smallpox in Brazil. In 1827, 900,000 people died of cholera in Europe. In 1877, 1 million people starved to death in China alone, and in 1918, 30 million people died during a worldwide epidemic of influenza.

The point here is that, according to the Bible, a calamity is coming unlike any that this world has ever seen. Jesus states in Matthew 24:21, "For then shall be great Tribulation, such as was not since the beginning of the world to this time, no, nor ever shall be." During this seven-year period, God will pour out upon the earth 21 judgments and three woes (Revelation 8:13).

The judgments start in Revelation 6 with the seven seal judgments. This is commonly known as the four horsemen of the Apocalypse. The first, the rider on the white horse, is none other than the Antichrist, the one who will be here on earth during the seven-year period. He is against Christ. The second horse is a red horse, which is a symbol of war and sudden destruction. The third horse is a black horse, which signifies famine. The famine will be so severe it will take a day's wages to buy two pints of wheat. The fourth horse is the pale horse. It represents death. One-fourth of mankind will be killed during the fourth horse rider's reign.

The fifth seal judgment will be the martyred remnant. These are the ones who get saved during the Tribulation and are killed for their testimony (Revelation 20:4). The sixth seal judgment will be a physical change on the earth. There will be no rain. People will flee to the mountains to hide from God's wrath.

The seventh seal is opened, which contains seven more judgments, known as the seven trumpet judgments. The first trumpet judgment will be a hailstorm and fire. One-third of all trees and green grass upon the earth will be burned up. The second trumpet judgment will be one-third of the sea will turn to blood. One-third of sea life will die. One-third of all ships sailing on the sea at that time will be destroyed. The third trumpet judgment will be one-third of the water will be turned to wormwood, and more death will result. The fourth trumpet judgment will be one-third of the sun, the moon, and the stars will be darkened, and then the three woes begin under this judgment. The fifth trumpet judgment will be the locusts that sting the unbelievers like scorpions. They will be tormented for five months. They will seek death but will not find it. This is the first woe.

The sixth trumpet judgment will be one-third of mankind will be killed. This is the second woe. Remember one-fourth have already been killed under the fourth seal judgment of the pale horse rider. The seventh trumpet judgment begins the last half of the Tribulation. There will be earthquakes and hailstorms. During this time there will be war in Heaven, and the devil will be cast out. This is the third woe. He comes down to earth and again begins His intense persecution of Israel for the last 3 1/2 years of the Tribulation. This is known as Jacob's Trouble. This starts the seven bowl or vial judgments.

These last seven judgments are filled with the wrath of God, according to Revelation 15:1. The judgments are intensified. The first bowl judgment will be painful sores upon all who have the mark of the Beast. The second will be the sea turning to blood. Every living thing in the sea dies. The third will be rivers and fountains will become all blood. The fourth will be the sun scorching men with fire. The fifth will be darkness and pain upon the earth. The sixth will be the Euphrates River drying up so that there will be a gathering of the world's armies to Armageddon. The seventh bowl judgment will be the greatest earthquake ever on the earth. Every mountain will be destroyed. Every island of the seas will flee away. Hailstorms will occur with the stones weighing 100 pounds each.

FACT 4 – Many people will be saved during the Tribulation.

Revelation 7 talks about the 144,000. This chapter is parenthetical; it is an interlude. The chapter does not contribute to the chronology of Revelation. It is put between the sixth and seventh seal judgments. No time or words will be wasted refuting the silly and unscriptural claim of the sect known as the Jehovah's Witnesses that brazenly claims that its group comprises this 144,000.

In Revelation 7:1-3 we see God takes time out to seal His servants during the Tribulation on this earth. What this sealing is we are told in Revelation 14:1. It's the Father's name on their foreheads. There is no secret discipleship. (So too will the Antichrist have his seal on his followers' foreheads. That seal will be the number 666.) Revelation 7:4-8 tells us the number that God will seal: 12,000 from each of the 12 tribes of Israel. God is going to seal 144,000 "Apostle Pauls," who will not bow a knee to the Antichrist. They will go forth over the earth and preach the gospel of the kingdom as prophesied in Matthew 24:14. They are going to accomplish in this short time period what the evangelical church has been trying to do during the last 2,000 years.

We read in the end of Revelation 7 that a great multitude of every nation, kindred, people, and tongue got saved, not only Jews. This is not the church. The church was raptured out before the Tribulation. These people got saved during the Great Tribulation (Revelation 14).

They will serve God in the heavenly temple. 1 Timothy 2:4 tells us that God would have all men be saved and come to the knowledge of the truth. Ezekiel 33:11 says God has "no pleasure in the death of the wicked." In fact, He gives to us (believers) great encouragement to be soul winners. Proverbs 11:30 says, "The fruit of the righteous is a tree of life; and he that winneth souls is wise."

Throughout these facts, I have been encouraging and teaching you that when you accept Christ as your Savior, the righteousness of Jesus Christ comes to rest upon you. God pronounces you a righteous person. When you accept Christ as your Savior, you now wear the "garments of salvation." God has placed upon you the "robe of righteousness" (Isaiah 61:10). Daniel 12:3 says, "And they that be wise (that is soul winners) shall shine as the brightness of the firmament; and they that turn many to righteousness (people who win someone to the Lord) as the stars for ever and ever."

In 1 Thessalonians 2:19 the Apostle Paul tells us that if you win one soul to the Lord, you will be given a crown of rejoicing. We are not talking about 1,000, 10,000, or 100,000 souls. We are talking about one soul. If you are involved in winning a soul to the Lord — that is talking to them, leading them to Christ, or praying for them to get saved, or witnessing to them, or inviting them to a church, and they get saved, you will receive this crown. Every Christian should desire to be a soul winner. You all know someone who needs to be saved. So how does one become a soul winner? You must ask God to make you a soul winner, to make you more sensitive to lost people around you, to open doors for you, to soften and tender hearts, to give you boldness, to give you knowledge of His Word. Prayer makes the difference. You can't talk to someone about the Lord until you first talk to the Lord about that someone.

FACT 5 – The Tribulation will be the time of the Antichrist.

This will be the time of the Antichrist, the Beast out of the sea of Revelation 13. Who is the Antichrist? This question is unanswerable and will remain unanswered until the Antichrist personally makes a covenant with Israel for seven years. This fact is according to the prophecy in Daniel 9:27.

The Book of Daniel is the premier prophecy book. Daniel 11 and 12 give a good description of the Antichrist. Let me give it to you. He will do according to his own will beginning in Daniel 11:21. He will exalt himself and magnify himself above every God. He will speak marvelous things against the God of gods. He will prosper till the indignation (the Tribulation) comes to an end. He will not regard the God of his fathers. He will honor a god his father's did not know. He will exist at the time of the end and be successful in his conquest. He will reign from Jerusalem. He will cause the greatest time of trouble ever on the earth. He will war with Israel. He will cause the abomination of desolation that Jesus Christ talks about in Matthew 24 and that has been prophesied in 2 Thessalonians 2:1-4. He will come to his end.

When will he be revealed? He cannot be revealed until the Rapture of the church takes place. 2 Thessalonians 2:6-8 says, "And now ye know what withholdeth that he might be revealed in his time (this is talking about the Antichrist). For the mystery of iniquity doth already work; only he who now letteth will let, until he be taken out of the way." This is talking about the Holy Spirit and the church as we are the restrainers of evil here on this earth. When we are taken out of the way, when we are raptured, the Antichrist will be revealed.

He is the rider of the white horse in Revelation 6:1-2. In the last 3 1/2 years of the Tribulation, he will exalt himself above God and will be worshipped by many. His power will come from Satan. Revelation 13:1 tells us, "And I stood upon the sand of the sea, and saw a beast rise up out of the sea (this is the Antichrist coming to this earth) having seven heads and ten horns, and upon his horns ten crowns, and upon his heads the name of blasphemy. And the beast which I saw was like unto a leopard, and his feet were as the feet of a bear, and his mouth as the mouth of a lion: and the dragon (that is the devil) gave him his power, and his seat, and great authority."

Revelation 13:7-8 says, "And it was given unto him to make war with the saints, and to overcome them. (This is talking about the Tribulation saints and is not talking about the church saints of today. We are not here. We have been raptured up to Heaven. He is making war with the Tribulation saints, or the people who got saved during the Tribulation from the preaching of the 144,000.) "And power was given him over all kindreds, and tongues, and nations. And all that dwell upon the earth shall worship him, whose names are not written in the Book of Life of the Lamb slain from the foundation of the world."

Satan has been, is now, and will be in one of the following locations. In the past he was in Heaven as God's anointed angel who rebelled against God (Ezekiel 28 and Isaiah 14). His present location is in Heaven as God's chief enemy. He is also around the world trafficking his rebellion up and down the highways and byways to deceive as many earthlings as he possibly can. That number is astronomical, and it is continually growing. In the future he will be on the earth as the guide for the Antichrist during the Tribulation. In the future he will be in the bottomless pit for almost 1,000 years during the millennial reign of Christ. Further into the future he will be let loose on the earth again for a short time at the end of the Millennium. Finally, his resting place will be in the Lake of Fire where he will be forever and ever.

The Antichrist will have the power to blaspheme God. He will have the power to overcome the Tribulation saints, to overcome the Jews, to conquer many nations, and to destroy mystery Babylon. He will have the power to overcome and kill God's two witnesses of Revelation 11. He will have the power to kill the 144,000 of Revelation 7. The Antichrist will be able to change times and laws. He will understand mysteries. He will have the power to protect the Jews as long as he desires, to make a covenant with them, to give them peace, to allow them to build their temple and to have temple worship. The Antichrist also will be able to work signs and wonders. He will be able to control money and riches in his own realm. He will have the power to curse and to cause great deception. He will be able to do according to his own will. The Antichrist will control religion and worship. He will control the lives of all men in his kingdom; he will control the kings. He will have the power to make all the nations fear him. Lastly, the Antichrist will have the power to fight against Christ.

The Bible gives him many names. His names are: Antichrist, the Assyrian, King of Babylon, the Spoiler, the Little Horn, the King of the North, the Man of Sin, the Son of Perdition, the Wicked One, and the Beast. He will possess the miraculous power of attracting people of every class, fascinating them with his marvelous personality, his successes, his wisdom, his administrative and executive ability and bringing them under his control through his well-directed flattery and master diplomacy. He will be endued with the power of Satan in the exercise of these gifts until the world will follow after him, and many will worship him.

However, with all these prophecies about his time, the Bible also gives us the prophecy of his end. 2 Thessalonians 2:8 says the Antichrist will be consumed and destroyed by the brightness of the Lord's coming." Revelation 19:20 says, the Antichrist will be cast into the Lake of Fire where he will be forever and ever.

FACT 6 – The Tribulation will be the time of Jacob's (the Jews') Trouble.

The reason for the Tribulation is to purify Israel and bring it to God, so He can fulfill the everlasting covenant He made with its fathers. The Tribulation also is a time when He will purify Israel and all rebels. God is going to plead during this time with Israel to bring them into the bond of the new covenant. He is also going to judge Israel and punish it for rejecting its Messiah. He is going to bring Israel to complete repentance.

This will be the time to fulfill the prophecy of Daniel. It will be the time when Israel will flee into the wilderness, so it will turn to God for help. It will be the time to judge the nations for their persecution of Israel and their denial of Christ as the only Savior. The Tribulation, though worldwide, will mainly concern Israel. The last 3 1/2 years will be the time of Jacob's (the Jews') trouble.

FACT 7 – The Tribulation will end with the battle of Armageddon.

All nations will be gathered north of Israel on the plains of Jezreel to come against Israel for her final destruction. At that time the Lord Jesus will come. The Second Coming will occur. We read in Matthew 24:27, "For as the lightning cometh out of the east and shineth even unto the west; so shall also the coming of the Son of man be." Lightning is very powerful and highly visible. If you close your eyes on a dark night during a thunder and lightning storm, you can still see the flashes of lightning while your eyes are closed.

Verse 28 says, "For wheresoever the carcass is, there will the eagles be gathered." Jesus is coming to end the Tribulation and to destroy all those armies that have come against Israel at the battle of Armageddon. Verse 29 says, "Immediately after the Tribulation of those days shall the sun be darkened, and the moon shall not give her light, and the stars shall fall from heaven, and the powers of the heavens shall be shaken." His coming will bring cataclysmic changes in the heavens. The entire universe will be thrown into total disarray. In verse 30 we read, "And then shall appear the sign of the Son of man in Heaven: and then shall all the tribes of the earth mourn, and they shall see the Son of man coming in the clouds of Heaven with power and great glory."

His coming will be visible. He will not come as a thief in the night this time, but every eye will see Him. Verse 31 says, "And He shall send his angels with a great sound of a trumpet, and they shall gather together his elect from the four winds, from one end of Heaven to the other." Just as the trumpets sounded to call us (believers) up to meet Jesus in the air at the Rapture, the trumpets will sound in Heaven to gather us (believers who have been raptured into Heaven) together to meet the Lord and return with Him to this earth at His Second Coming. And we shall ever be with the Lord throughout the 1,000 years of His reign and throughout all eternity.

In this chapter I have talked about the wrath of God to come, according to the Bible. Great calamities have occurred on this earth but never as great and horrible as the wrath of God that will come upon the whole world during the seven-year Tribulation period.

I thank God that the believing church will be saved from the wrath to come (1 Thessalonians 1:10, 1 Thessalonians 5:9, Romans 5:9 — this verse is in the future tense). As believers we are to be "Looking for that blessed hope, and the glorious appearing of the great God and our Saviour Jesus Christ; Who gave Himself for us (Titus 2:13-14). It certainly would not be a blessed hope if we were to go through any part of the seven-year Tribulation period and suffer God's wrath upon a world that rejected Him when we accepted Him and believed in Him. "When the plain sense of Scripture makes common sense, seek no other sense." And this makes common sense that God will save believers from His coming wrath.

CHAPTER 16 | FACTS 106-112

7 Facts About
The Millennium

FACT 1 – Believers will stand before the Judgment Seat of Christ during the Tribulation and just before the Millennium.

Every believer from the time of the Cross until the Rapture will be taken bodily up to Heaven and will stand before the judgment seat of Christ. Romans 14:10 tells us, "But why dost thou judge thy brother? or why dost thou set at nought thy brother? For we shall all stand before the judgment seat of Christ." 2 Corinthians 5:10 tells us, "For we must all appear before the judgment seat of Christ; that every one may receive the things done in his body, according to that he hath done, whether it be good or bad."

1 Corinthians 3:10-16 says, "According to the grace of God which is given unto me, as a wise masterbuilder, I have laid the foundation, and another buildeth thereon. But let every man take heed how he buildeth thereupon. For other foundation can no man lay than that is laid, which is Jesus Christ. Now if any

man build upon this foundation gold, silver, precious stones, wood, hay, stubble; every man's work shall be made manifest: for the day shall declare it, because it shall be revealed by fire; and the fire shall try every man's work of what sort it is. If any man's work abide which he hath built there upon, he shall receive a reward. If any man's work shall be burned, he shall suffer loss: but he himself shall be saved; yet so as by fire. Know ye not that ye are the temple of God, and that the Spirit of God dwelleth in you?"

Here the Bible is talking about rewards. Remember there is "now no condemnation to them which are in Christ Jesus (Romans 8:1). Salvation is a free gift. Rewards are earned by works. The Bible's way is salvation first and works second. Works are an outward religious service. It is the expression and proof of faith. We are to be "doers of the word, and not hearers only" (James 1:22). James is saying (my paraphrase), "You show me a man with little works, and I'll show you a man of little faith. On the other hand, you show me a man with much or many works, and I'll show you a man of great faith."

In believer's works, gifts come into play, and you need to find your gift and use it for the Lord. We can obtain five rewards in Heaven. They are called crowns. Revelation 2:10 says, "Be thou faithful unto death, and I will give thee a crown of life." This is a crown for those who have endured testing and trials for their faith. It is called the martyr's crown.

In 1 Corinthians 9:25 we find a second crown: "And every man that striveth for the mastery is temperate in all things. Now they do it to obtain a corruptible crown; but we an incorruptible." This is a crown for faithful stewardship, giving of your money, time, and talents to the Lord.

The third crown that is found in the Scriptures is in 1 Peter 5:2, "Feed the flock." Two verses later, the Bible says, "And when the chief Shepherd shall appear (that's Jesus), ye shall receive a crown of glory that fadeth not away." This is a crown for leadership. It's given to pastors, elders, teachers, and so forth, who faithfully adhered to and taught the principles of the Word of God and have not compromised them.

The fourth crown is found in 1 Thessalonians 2:19, "For what is our hope, or joy, or crown of rejoicing? Are not even ye in the presence of our Lord Jesus Christ at his coming?" Paul is writing about people he has won to the Lord, and he will rejoice to see them in the presence of the Lord at His coming. This is the crown for soul winning. This is for those who lead people to the Lord, who pray for people to get saved and they receive the Lord, who invite people to church and they get saved, who live a testimony before the world, and people are led to the Lord through their testimony.

The fifth crown is found in 2 Timothy 4:8: "Henceforth there is laid up for me a crown of righteousness, which the Lord, the righteous judge, shall give me at that day: and not to me only, but unto all them also that love His appearing." This is a crown for a life of loyal service to our Lord. This is for missionaries and also for those of us who are looking for the blessed hope and the glorious appearing of the great God and our Savior, the Lord Jesus Christ, who loved us and "gave Himself for us, that he might redeem us from all iniquity, and purify unto Himself a peculiar people, zealous of good works" (Titus 2:14).

After the judgment seat of Christ, we, the church, will be married to the Lord Jesus Christ. We will become His bride, and we will return with Him to this earth (Matthew 24:27-31). Jesus, at His return, will go to Petra, where the Jewish remnant will accept Him as their Messiah. He will come through the Eastern Gate of the temple, and for 75 days, he will judge the nations (Matthew 25:32) and the nation of Israel. Then the 1,000 years, known as the Millennium, will begin.

FACT 2 – After His return to this earth, Christ will set up His Kingdom.

The Kingdom will last for 1,000 years. Satan will be bound during this time. This time periods will be the answer to the Lord's prayer in Matthew 6:10 when He prayed, "Thy kingdom come, Thy will be done in earth, as it is in Heaven." Christ will redeem creation that Adam gave over to Satan when he disobeyed and rebelled against his God. Christ now gets it back. The Millennium will fulfill biblical prophecy. It will be a theocratic government. Christ will be the King of Kings and Lord of Lords as He rules and reigns. It will be a holy kingdom with perfect justice, protection, and freedom from oppression. "The earth shall be full of the knowledge of the Lord, as the waters cover the sea" during this time (Isaiah 11:9).

FACT 3 – The redeemed throughout all the ages will be here for the 1,000 years helping Christ rule (Isaiah 35:9-10 and Isaiah 51:11).

Redeemed means *to be bought out of the marketplace*. The Greek word for it is *exagoratzo*. It is when Jesus Christ left the glories of Heaven and came here to this earth. We were looked upon as slaves to sin, and Jesus Christ came into the marketplace and bought us out of it. In other words, He extracts us from this marketplace of sin. He redeems us. We are redeemed with the precious blood of the Lord Jesus Christ.

FACT 4 – A great environmental change will take place during the 1,000 years.

Most Bible scholars believe the earth will revert back to how it was before the flood when the climate was universally warm, pleasant, and mild. There were no deserts or ice caps. There was more land surface than there is today. There were no rugged mountains or deep canyons. There was worldwide lush vegetation. The Millennium will be a time when there will be an increase in light. The moon will be as bright as the sun, and the sun will be seven times brighter than it is now (Isaiah 30:26).

FACT 5 – No unsaved person will enter into the Millennium.

Millions of babies will be born during the Millennium. They will be born to saved Israelite and Gentile parents, who survived the Tribulation and entered the Millennium in a state of mortality. As beautiful and perfect as the Millennium will be, it will not be Heaven. Sin will be possible during the 1,000 years. People will refuse to submit their hearts to the new birth. We are born with a sin nature. A perfect environment will not take away sin. Just because we are children of saved parents, we still have a sin nature. Salvation does not come through genetics. The Lord is immutable. He never changes (Malachi 3:6). We must be born again. Christ will rule with a rod of iron during the Millennium.

FACT 6 – People during the Millennium will have to worship the Lord.

Every year they will have to worship the Lord of Hosts and keep the Feast of Tabernacles (Zechariah 14:16 and Deuteronomy 16:13). The Feast of Tabernacles is a seven-day feast to praise and rejoice in what God has given them in the past year.

FACT 7 – The Millennium will end with Satan being loosed from the bottomless pit for a season.

He will go forth to tempt the nations to turn them against Christ. Revelation 20:7-15 says, "And when the thousand years are expired, Satan shall be loosed out of his prison, and shall go out to deceive the nations which are in the four quarters of the earth, Gog and Magog, to gather them together to battle: the number of whom is as the sand of the sea. And they went up on the breadth of the earth, and compassed the camp of the saints about, and the beloved city: and fire came down from God out of Heaven, and devoured them. And the devil that deceived them was cast into the lake of fire and brimstone, where the beast and the false prophet are, and shall be tormented day and night for ever and ever. And I saw a great white throne, and Him that sat on it, from whose face the earth and the Heaven fled away; and there was found no place for them. And I saw the dead, small and great, stand before God; and the books were opened: and another book was opened, which is the *Book of Life*: and the dead were judged out of those things which were written in the books, according to their works. And the sea gave up the dead which were in it; and death and hell delivered up the dead which were in them: and they were judged every man according to their works. And death and hell were cast into the lake of fire. This is the second death. And whosoever was not found written in the *Book of Life* was cast into the lake of fire."

This great white throne judgment is a judgment of the wicked dead. These are the spiritually dead, the people who rejected the Lord Jesus Christ as their personal Savior. This is all unbelievers, all unsaved people from the time of Adam until the present time. We will see the small and the great, that's beggars and kings, stand in judgment before God.

The Bible says the books will be opened: the *Book of Conscience*, the *Book of Words*, the *Book of Secrets*, the *Book of Outward Deeds*, and the *Book of Life*. The Bible will be opened, and those whose names are not found written in the *Book of Life* will be cast into the lake of fire (Revelation 20:15). My concern and my question for you at this time: Are you sure your name is written in the *Lamb's Book of Life*? We read in Revelation 21:27, "And there shall in no wise enter into it any thing that defileth, neither whatsoever worketh abomination, or maketh a lie (talking about entering into Heaven): but they which are written in the *Lamb's Book of Life*" will enter into Heaven."

Is your name in the *Lamb's Book of Life?*

CHAPTER 17 | FACTS 113-119

7 Facts About
Heaven

Did you know an indescribably, wonderful experience awaits you? If you are a child of God, a day is coming when you will be raptured off of this earth, or you will close your eyes to all the familiar scenes of this earth and immediately open them to the rapturous beauty of God's celestial homeland we call Heaven.

You might have had many thrilling experiences here and traveled to far-off places and seen magnificent, beautiful landscapes, but all these things will seem as nothing the moment you set foot in the brilliance and the unbelievable splendor of God's paradise. No words can describe this most wonderful place.

If all the thrills of this life were wrapped up into one huge thrill, it would not even be worthy of comparison to the thrill that will envelope your heart when you look upon God's throne. We will be absolutely lost in wonder and amazement. Far too many people have not understood that this life is brief compared with eternity.

The Bible tells us we are to be but strangers and pilgrims here on this earth. We are journeying across the pages of time with one purpose in mind, to reach that City that has foundations whose builder and maker is God (Hebrews 11:10). A tent or a cottage, why should I care? He is building a palace for me over there.

Life does have a purpose, and that purpose is to make sure of our Heavenly destiny. God never intended that this time should be an end in itself. We are to serve God faithfully here on earth so that He may reward us bountifully up in Heaven. In a very real sense, what we do here determines what we are up there. Time passes swiftly. All too soon the days of our life will be gone.

Now is the time to prepare for Heaven. Today is the day for commitment, steadfastness, and loyal service for Christ. Now is the time we should walk as He walks. Remember one life will soon be past; only what we do for Christ will last. There is a reason behind all things. God has a great master plan in everything He has done. As we look through God's eyes, we can see that all things are steadily progressing toward God's planned climax.

Life has a goal, and that goal is not merely a grave in which to rest after life's trials are over. Life's goal is Heaven; a glorious, never-ending Heaven. That's what makes the subject of Heaven so important. Everything is moving that way. Heaven is the grand culmination of all of life's desires. "The sufferings of this present time are not worthy to be compared with the glory which shall be revealed in us" someday in Heaven (Romans 8:18). Life is incomplete without a knowledge of Heaven.

Some things can be known about Heaven. When we know these our hearts overflow with joy, and our souls are completely satisfied with eternal assurance. Here are seven facts about Heaven.

7 FACTS ABOUT HEAVEN

FACT 1 – Heaven is a real place.

It's just like New York City or Chicago or London or Paris are real places.

FACT 2 – Heaven is up.

Jesus went up (Mark 16:19). Paul was called up into Heaven (2 Corinthians 12:2). John was told to "Come up hither" (Revelation 4:1). I also can tell you that Heaven seems to be in the north. Isaiah 14:13 says Lucifer in his rebellion against God said he would "sit also upon the mount of the congregation, in the side of the north."

FACT 3 – Heaven is for righteous people only.

When you accepted Christ as your Savior, God placed to your account the righteousness of the Lord Jesus Christ. You became a righteous person. In Matthew 25:46, Jesus said, "And these shall go away into everlasting punishment: but the righteous into life eternal."

FACT 4 – Heaven is a place of bliss.

What a marvelous place Heaven is going to be! It seems almost too good to be true. God has promised a home in Heaven to all those who have accepted and put their faith and trust in Jesus as their Savior. All the glories of Heaven will be yours. "Eye hath not seen, nor ear heard, neither have entered into the heart of man, the things which God hath prepared for them that love Him (1 Corinthians 2:9). We will dwell with Christ in heavenly bliss forever. I knew a very fine brother in the Lord. His name is Professor Earl Chuty, and when he was preaching about Heaven, he used these words. "How woooooonnnnnnddddderrrrrfff-fuuuuulllll Heaven is going to be!"

FACT 5 – We will know each other in Heaven.

We are going to know our spouses, our children, our family, and our friends. We will know all those who accepted Jesus Christ.

FACT 6 – There will be a lot of "no more's" in Heaven.

There will be no more sickness or pain, no more anxiety (Revelation 21:4). There will be no more sin. You will never hurt the heart of God. There will be no more death, and there will be no more separation. No more will you be separated from loved ones.

FACT 7 – Heaven is forever.

God inhabits eternity. Eternity has no beginning or ending. It's endless. There is no time in eternity. As the bride of Christ, we will dwell in the new city. It will be a spacious city; 1,400 plus miles square and 1,400 plus miles high. I believe it will be a spacious cube. Dr. David Jeremiah writes, "To grasp something of the enormity of the heavenly city, consider this: That it is 40 times the area of England, 20 times that of New Zealand, and 10 times the area of Germany or France." The ground floor is two-thirds the size of the United States. It would provide enough living space for far more people than have ever lived in the history of the world. And that is just the first floor. There are 1,400 plus miles of floors above it.

Psalm 23:6 tells us we will "dwell in the house of the Lord for ever." And 1 Thessalonians 4:17 ends with, "So shall we ever be with the Lord."

CHAPTER 18 | FACT 120

Fact 120
The Most Important Fact of All

Before I give you this fact, I want to thank you for reading my book. I hope you have gained some facts about the Bible. I have tried to give you facts on many biblical topics about which people want to know. Of all the facts I have given you, this 120th fact is the most important. It is from my heart to your heart. It is where your feet meet the street.

Most people are concerned about their lives, their everyday lives, and they should be. This fact is about the end of your life. It's about your eternal destiny. We never know when our life will end. In fact, most people don't think about death. However, the Bible says, "It is appointed unto men once to die (Hebrews 9:27). Do you know anyone who has lived forever?

God loves all the people of the world: red and yellow, black and white, they are precious in His sight. God is long-suffering. He wants everyone to come to the knowledge of the truth. What is the truth? The truth is that everyone, including you and I, has been born with a sin nature. Think about it. No one taught us to have evil thoughts, words, and deeds. We have these because it's natural to us. All these wrong things we do are sin to God because He is a righteous God, and sin is what separates us from God.

Because God loves us so much, He sent His only begotten, sinless Son to this earth to die on the Cross for our sin. 2 Corinthians 5:21 tells us, "For he hath made him (Jesus) to be sin for us, who knew no sin; that we might be made the righteousness of God in Him. You see, Jesus took your sin and my sin upon Himself and died on the Cross for us, so God can forgive us of our sins.

When a person comes to realize he or she is a sinner and Jesus died on the Cross for their sins, they come to the knowledge of the truth. When a person accepts Jesus Christ into their heart as their personal Savior, God forgives them of their sin and gives them eternal life in Heaven (this is life after death).

I remember when I came to the knowledge of the truth. I was 12 years old and was attending a release time after school. Two Christian ladies told me about Jesus, and I accepted Him into my heart as my Savior.

I certainly wish you would consider this last fact, and you would realize as I did that you need to accept Jesus into your heart as your own personal Savior. This is not a hard thing to do, and it is the most important thing you will ever do in your life.

Please, won't you make Jesus your Savior? All you have to do is pray this prayer in sincerity, and God will save you:

THE MOST IMPORTANT FACT OF ALL

Heavenly Father, I believe that Jesus Christ your Son died on the Cross for my sin. I believe in my heart that you have raised Him from the dead. Father I confess to you that I am a sinner. I ask that you will be merciful to me, a sinner, and save me for Jesus' sake. I accept Jesus Christ into my heart as my personal Savior. Help me to live for Him all the days of my life. In the name of the Lord Jesus Christ I pray. Amen.

I thank the Lord for you. If you prayed this prayer, I would appreciate if you would write to me about your decision, and I also will pray for you.

Thank you again so much for reading my book.

Don Klinger
P.O. Box 342
Millersburg, PA 17061

Made in the USA
Middletown, DE
16 April 2015